# What Makes Winning Brands Different?

# *What Makes Winning Brands Different?*

## The Hidden Method Behind the World's Most Successful Brands

ANDREAS BUCHHOLZ • WOLFRAM WÖRDEMANN

JOHN WILEY & SONS, LTD

Chichester · New York · Weinheim · Brisbane · Singapore · Toronto

Originally published under the title Was Siegermarken anders machen, by Econ Verlag, an imprint of Verlagshaus Goethestrasse GmbH & Co. KG. (1998).

Updated and revised edition published in Germany under the title Der Wachstumscode für Siegermarken (2000).

This edition translated by J. Derek Brennan.

*Other Wiley Editorial Offices*

John Wiley & Sons, Inc., 605 Third Avenue,
New York, NY 10158-0012, USA

WILEY-VCH GmbH, Pappelallee 3,
D-69469 Weinheim, Germany

Jacaranda Wiley Ltd, 33 Park Road, Milton,
Queensland 4064, Australia

John Wiley & Sons (Asia) Pte Ltd, 2 Clementi Loop #02-01,
Jin Xing Distripark, Singapore 129809

John Wiley & Sons (Canada) Ltd, 22 Worcester Road,
Rexdale, Ontario M9W 1L1, Canada

*British Library Cataloguing in Publication Data*
A catalogue record for this book is available from the British Library

ISBN 0-471-72025-9

Typeset in Bodoni Book by Best-set Typesetter Ltd., Hong Kong.
Printed and bound in Great Britain by Bookcraft (Bath) Ltd, Midsomer Norton, Somerset.
This book is printed on acid-free paper responsibly manufactured from sustainable forestry, in which at least two trees are planted for each one used for paper production.

## DEDICATION

To Arnold. To Zdenka. To Kathy.

# C O N T E N T S

# ACKNOWLEDGMENTS

We would like to acknowledge the immense help and assistance of J. Derek Brennan whose tireless efforts were invaluable in the preparation of this manuscript. His astute observations, international insights and substantial contributions, along with constant prodding have added depth to our analysis and kept it on track. Quite frankly, Derek's professional knowledge and writing style have added a quality to this book we had not expected to achieve. Although the many occasions we have had to work together on developing winning strategies have always been inspiring and rewarding, the days spent at his home on Marstrand in the final stages of this book will remain an especially fond memory.

J. Derek Brennan is a marketing and communications consultant working with agencies and advertisers in Europe and the United States. He lives on Marstrand, an island off the West Coast of Sweden, with Ashton, his Irish Setter.

## S O M E T H I N G    N E W

In this book you will for the first time read about *growth codes*: proven, workable principles for developing the *optimum positioning* for your brand. You can apply them to any product, any service in any business or industry to increase sales and market share reliably.

What is behind it? Over six years of continuous research on more than 1000 winning brands. They are the best of the best in all markets and industries, having consistently achieved double-digit – and in some cases even triple-digit – growth. We wanted to find out what these winning brands do differently from the legions out there battling for growth but getting nowhere or getting there slowly. What is it that makes them click with the consumer?

The result of this extensive research is *growth codes* that can be applied in a practical, systematic manner to overcome even the most challenging marketing odds and set virtually any brand on a new path to growth.

- How can a fruit juice suddenly experience a growth rate of 35% even though the consumer finds it more watery, sweeter and more artificial than 100% pure juice products?

- How does a new small car become an enduring best seller although it looks like a shoebox on wheels?

- How can a pasta brand without any objective quality advantage achieve market dominance against 400 competitors in the same market?

These and other spectacular successes were achieved by infusing the brand with a specific growth code. The following pages will introduce you to a new way of developing sure-fire strategies that will result in higher sales and market share for *any* brand.

Enjoy the read.
*Andreas Buchholz*
*Wolfram Wördemann*

## O V E R V I E W

## THE ROAD TO A NEW METHOD

How we discovered the *growth codes* for addressing powerful purchase motives in the consumer's mind.

## PORTAL 1: BENEFITS & PROMISES

How to identify and shape a compelling *virtual* edge over competitors.

## PORTAL 2: NORMS & VALUES

How to appeal to your consumer's sense of duty, pride and morals.

## PORTAL 3: PERCEPTIONS & PROGRAMS

How to transform your brand in the consumer's perception.

## PORTAL 4: IDENTITY & SELF-EXPRESSION

How to make your brand the "megaphone" for what the consumer wants to express.

## PORTAL 5: EMOTIONS & LOVE

How to generate feelings so powerful that consumers will buy your brand out of *love*.

## WORKING WITH GROWTH CODES

How the blw method can help you solve even the most daunting marketing challenges.

## TAKING GROWTH CODES INTO THE INTERNET AGE

How the blw method maximizes knowledge management.

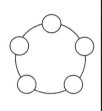 # The Road to a New Method

## THE MARKETING MELTDOWN

When you step into a supermarket today, you probably do not realize that besides the 20 or so brands you are interested in, there are about 30000 brands interested in *you*. And that is only a fraction of all the products and services out there that are trying to win your business every day.

World wide the product universe is expanding – it has doubled from what it was just two decades ago – while the consumer universe is shrinking. Low or negative birthrates in the United States, Europe and Japan will reduce the number of consumers by half within the next two generations. Although new markets are gaining momentum – China, India, Africa as well as Latin and South America – they are not growing quickly enough to absorb the brand glut forming on the horizon (Insead University, Fontainebleau, France).

More and more products for fewer and fewer consumers – that is only the first aspect of the marketing meltdown. The second is the fact that products and services are becoming more and more *interchangeable*. Often it is virtually impossible to identify a selling point on the basis of objective quality factors. What is it that differentiates competing detergents, facial tissues or stereo systems? Let us not even get into cigarettes, mineral water or beer. A recent survey of top executives from German breweries proved an embarrassing experience for them: they were unable to identify their own beer brand in a blindfold test (*Spiegel*, 37/97). If the people who make the product cannot tell the difference, how on earth can those who buy it? No wonder *price* is often the differentiating criterion. Currently discount chains and generic brands are experiencing the strongest growth worldwide.

As if interchangeable products caught in a price crunch were not enough, the third aspect behind the marketing meltdown is not encouraging either: *information overload*. In the United States, the number of TV stations has increased from 96 in 1950 to 1216 in 1999. During the same period, media expenditures for advertising have increased by a factor of more than 1000: from US$170 *million* in 1950 to US$210 *billion* in 1999. However, this staggering development of the media landscape is leading to only a marginal increase in media usage. One survey, for instance, shows that American households with more than 80 TV channels on average watch only 15 of them. In other words, four out of five channels are being tuned out (Television Bureau of Advertising, 1998). The consumer is being flooded with information in quantities that are impossible to digest. Scientists estimate that the average person today registers at most 2% to 3% of the aggregate information they are bombarded with every day (Professor Kroeber-Riel, University of Saarbrücken, Germany).

Countless brands out there fail in the marketplace for all these good reasons. Between 40% and 60% of those that are introduced into the market disappear within the first year (*Lebensmittel-Praxis*: Extra 3/97, Frankfurt, 1997) Not surprisingly, figures on the effectiveness of advertising campaigns are similarly dismal.

Renowned marketing authority John Philip Jones found that only 46% percent of 2000 brand campaigns surveyed in the United States had a positive effect on sales over a period of 12 months. This means that 54% of the investment made in brand communications – more than US$100 billion – evaporates without a return. In other words, every brand campaign has a 50–50 chance of success. Might as well flip a coin.

This is the bleak marketing reality of today. Not only in the United States, but also in practically all the western market economies. But there is also some good news . . .

## THE INKLING OF AN IDEA

There are brands in all markets and industries that are not only successful, but are also growing from strength to strength against these odds. Some even become multibillion-dollar assets, as *The Financial World*'s annual brand ranking for 1997 shows (Table 1.1). Obviously, it pays to get it right. . . .

Bear in mind that this table only assesses *brand* value, not the value of the *company* behind the brand. These figures therefore do not include any other assets. The table only indicates the pure brand value that impacts the bottom line at the end of every fiscal year.

But why should we focus on the world's *biggest* brands? There are other brands in every country and in every industry that are also achieving two- to three-digit growth rates. In relative terms they are superbrands in their own right.

To summarize, on the one hand we have a marketing meltdown that is whipping at least 50% of all brands. On the other, we have a very select group of top performers that achieve meteoric growth. This begs one question: What makes winning brands different? The search for the answer is what has driven an extensive research effort over the past few years. . . .

Table 1.1   *The Financial World*'s annual brand ranking, 1997.

| Product | Brand value in US$ (millions) |
| --- | --- |
| Coca-Cola | 48 000 |
| Marlboro | 47 600 |
| McDonald's | 19 900 |
| Walt Disney | 17 100 |
| Sony | 14 700 |
| Kodak | 14 400 |
| Intel | 13 300 |
| Gillette | 12 000 |
| Budweiser | 12 000 |
| Nike | 11 100 |
| Kellogg's | 10 700 |
| Nescafé | 10 300 |
| Pepsi | 9 300 |
| Levi's | 8 200 |

**Our idea:** *to distill the experience of the world's most successful brands and see what triggered their growth.*

Winning brands are indeed sitting on an invaluable wealth of experience – a mother lode of pure gold waiting to be mined. Yet so far the world's best brands have never been surveyed systematically. Our intention is to extract the essence of their success and transform it into an effective, easy-to-use tool. Our focus is on the top fifth percentile of all the brands that *effectively* have achieved outstanding successes in the market. Every year, they have grown consistently by 10%, 30%, even 50% and more. So, what is so different about these winning brands? Excellent quality cannot be the only explanation. The less successful competitors of Marlboro, Levi's, Nike, Budweiser or Kodak no doubt also make excellent products. The secret of winning brands must lie somewhere else. And it is doubtful that they are just luckier than others in flipping a coin.

Why has the success of winning brands never been analyzed before? Simple: where do you start with brands that are so diverse from each other that a common denominator seems impossible to define? What do a video game, a cruise line and a cat litter have in common – besides of course, the staggering success in their respective markets. Imagine standing in front of row upon row of fat binders that contain the success stories of more than 1000 brands. How would you proceed to find the common success denominator? Impossible, many would say, because these are 1000 individual cases – 1000 *specific* products or services, each faced with a *specific* market situation and each aimed at a *specific* consumer group. There is little sense in cataloguing, be it alphabetically, by industry, country or consumer groups. We need to dig deeper.

**Our approach:** *to find out how winning brands address a purchase motive in the consumer's mind. In other words:* **how** *do they click with the consumer?*

Obviously, any brand that grows addresses a compelling purchase motive – be it rational, psychological or emotional. Conversely, even the strongest brand core is useless if it does not click with consumers.

So, *how* do winning brands do it?

## DETECTIVE WORK

Our investigation spans six years and covers 1045 winning brands, each one ranked in the top fifth percentile of its industry in terms of growth. They represent the tip of an iceberg consisting of more than 20000 brands. All important industries are represented:

- Food
- Non-food (both consumables and non-consumables)
- Investment goods, and
- Services.

We ferreted out winning brands from around the globe – from the United States, Europe, South America, Asia and Australia. They have all won effectiveness awards and are the subject of case studies published by marketing institutes, trade publications and textbooks. Their exceptional growth is documented.

A number of international consumption goods manufacturers have graciously accepted to provide us with internal data about their own winning brands (although in most instances we will supply the data to corroborate growth claims, we cannot do this in all cases for reasons of confidentiality).

We consciously opted for a *cross-industry* approach to brand analysis. Why? Because looking for success factors *within one and the same* industry would have unnecessarily restricted our perspective and cheated us out of interesting parallels and new insights. Hundreds of car, detergent and beer brands around the world come across as painfully interchangeable. And that is no wonder because they keep looking for answers within the limited scope of their own industry. The result is "marketing incest." The first step toward new Big Ideas is to open your mind to fresh perspectives and angles from other industries. Many large corporations have already begun a process of cross-fertilization. Kraft Jacobs Suchard hires brand experts from the cigarette industry. Marketing executives from Coca-Cola are now working at DaimlerChrysler. The *products* are different, but the *marketing* challenge is similar: it is all about clicking with the consumer.

## UNCOVERING GROWTH CODES

After many thousands of hours we now have a clear picture of what winning brands do differently.

**The discovery:** *Winning brands adhere to specific laws when they activate a purchase motive in the consumer's mind. These laws are universal, applicable to any product or service in any market. We call them* **growth codes.**

Growth codes will identify a compelling purchase motive for an average beer brand just as systematically and effectively as for a car brand that is losing market share, or an insurance company that your consumer perceives as too expensive.

That is just theory, you say. Here is an example of how it works in practice.

It becomes clear that a growth code is not one *specific* solution for one *specific* brand in one *specific* market. The success of the Migration Principle can be replicated in all industries – foods, consumer products, investment goods, services or institutions.

---

### Your Mission: To Market a Fruit Juice

1. *The problem*: Your fruit juice is losing market share. Market research tells you that your beverage is more watery, sweeter, more artificial and less fruity than 100% juices. In other words, there is no clear purchase motive. How do you turn this product into a strong, growing brand within just a few months? Where do you even *begin* to look for a solution? Think about it for a minute . . .

2. *The growth code*: Working the problem from a growth code perspective directs us to the Migration

Principle: *"Migrate into a different or even unexpected 'mental drawer' where your brand can better unfold."* (cf. Portal 3: Perceptions & Programs)

3. *Applying the code*: Consumers have so far assigned us to the mental drawer of juice and rightfully compared us with 100% fruit juices. Now our job is to place our brand into a *different* mental drawer, sparking new brand growth. But which one? The most promising candidate is *soft drinks*! And here are the success factors:

   - *Acceptance:* Will consumers accept the product as a soft drink? Here, the fact that it is not as thick as 100% juices actually strengthens the case.

   - *Potential:* Does the new mental drawer offer better growth opportunities than the current market? The answer is "yes" here, too: the soft drink market is up to 10 times larger than the 100% fruit juice category.

   - *Uniqueness:* What will differentiate the brand in the new category and give it a unique edge? Our brand is now *less* watery, *not as* sweet, *less* artificial, and contains *more* fruit than other *soft drinks*.

   Conclusion: We have achieved a complete turn-around. The same characteristics that registered as negatives in the initial mental drawer now add up to compelling benefits in our new, larger market.

4. *The bottom line*: Sales go up 35% per year (we know this because this is an authentic case study).

One single growth code can create new growth for countless different types of brands. The following chapters will introduce you to 26 additional growth codes that are equally effective in clicking with the consumer.

## THE b|w METHOD

The growth codes form the basis of a new approach to brand marketing that we call the Buchholz–Wördemann (b|w) method. We have just hinted at how it is applied. But how do we figure out which growth code to apply? To simplify the search process, we arrange them behind five portals in the consumer's mind (Figure 1.1):

1. Benefits & Promises
2. Norms & Values
3. Perceptions & Programs
4. Identity & Self-expression
5. Emotions & Love

Let us take a peek behind each one of these doors. . . .

### Portal 1: Benefits & Promises

**Premise:** *Consumers prefer your brand because it offers a compelling (virtual) benefit.*

Very often consumers swear by "their" beer or "their" laundry detergent – although there is no evidence of superior quality. How can your brand achieve the same status in the consumer's choice? The challenge is to *create a compelling virtual benefit.* We will introduce you to five growth codes that will make your brand the logical choice to the consumer.

Benefits and promises are not the only reasons people choose one brand over another. There are four other portals to powerful purchase motives.

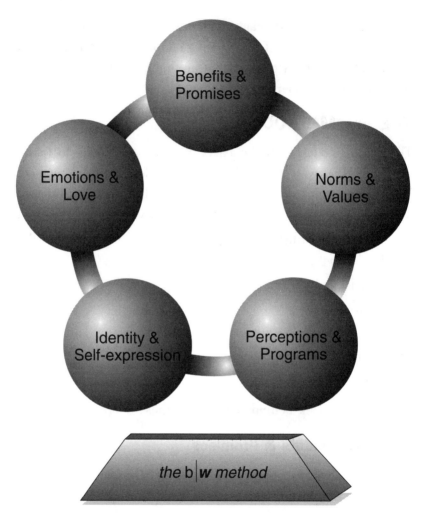

Figure 1. The five portals to your consumer's mind

## Portal 2: Norms & Values

**Premise:** *Consumers prefer your brand because it resolves an inner conflict (with their norms and values).*

Norms and values dictate much of our behavior from morning to night, throughout our lives. They always come into play when we do or don't do something out of a sense of duty, responsibility, pride, gratitude or shame. Norms and values naturally also impact our purchase decisions. Your brand can, for instance

- eliminate existing feelings of guilt,
- challenge – and satisfy – a consumer's pride, or even
- neutralize taboos connected with your product,

to name just a few of the possibilities for new and unexpected paths to growth.

## Portal 3: Perceptions & Programs

**Premise:** *Consumers prefer your brand because perception and behavior programs point to it as a logical choice.*

The way we perceive things is the result of programs deeply ingrained in our minds. Think of pigeonholing, for instance. But what does that have to do with increasing your market share? Imagine a cough drop brand that consumers keep stored in the mental drawer for *cough medication* – which means it is only purchased when cough symptoms appear. Now what if we placed it in the mental drawer for *candy*? Gone are the limitations of being perceived solely as appropriate in case of a cold or flu. The success of your brand largely depends on the mental drawer you are in.

## Portal 4: Identity & Self-expression

**Premise:** *Consumers prefer your brand because it expresses their (desired) character and identity.*

Brands help consumers define their identity and express it outwardly. This applies not only to clothing brands, but also practically to all outwardly visible characteristics of the consumer. The car you drive, the paper you have tucked under your arm, the watch on your wrist, the detergent you put on the belt in front of the cashier – they all demonstrate the *characterizing* power of a brand. Within a split-second, a brand can draw a complete picture of the consumer's character, personality and identity. Winning brands express precisely that personality or character trait which the consumer aspires to most.

## Portal 5: Emotions & Love

**Premise:** *Consumers prefer your product or service because they* **love** *the brand.*

There are *things* consumers simply "love." Think about a child's teddy bear or your own favorite sweater or a treasured memento. Products that are loved are not replaceable or interchangeable. What this tells us is that very powerful emotions can be attached to an object. They can also be attached to a brand. So many brands fail because they are satisfied with being *liked*. Winning brands are *loved*. "Like" is not enough – love is what keeps consumers loyal.

Now that we have described the five portals in the consumer's mind, let us take just one step back and look at the big picture. In other words, What is the bottom line?

# THE BIG OPPORTUNITY

Growth codes are universal – they can be applied to all products and services, in all countries, today and tomorrow. Why are we so sure? Because they involve rational, psychological and emotional processes within the mind that are common to all humans. It is the way humans tick, regardless of what we intend to buy – be it car, a laundry detergent or an insurance policy. Regardless of whether we are German, Chinese or Thai. Regardless of whether we go shopping today or our descendant goes shopping a thousand years from now. The way our minds process purchase decisions will not change.

This leads us to an important conclusion: growth codes are not bound by the specifics of your market or your consumers. These specifics, much like variables in an equation, enter into the picture as you *apply* growth codes to solving your marketing problem. The more you know about your product or service, your industry, consumers and competitors, and the better your grasp of trends and market changes, the more effective the growth code.

Let us cut to the chase: What exactly will this new method do for you?

*The b|w method offers a maximum of certainty in setting a course for new growth.*
(This applies to products, services and organizations of all kinds. Excluded are those brands that are evidently superfluous or distinctly inferior. The object of marketing is not to deceive the consumer.)

In other words, this is about the *security* of your brand investment. Can we offer absolute certainty? Is this a guaranteed solution for brand growth? There are no guarantees in life and none in marketing, but a systematic method can help achieve a maximum of certainty. Here are three reasons why.

1. *Tapping a vast, global knowledge base*: Growth codes are distilled from the successes of the world's winning brands. All the tried-and-tested strategic approaches, strokes of genius and inspired maneuvers are stored within them and are readily accessible. You can apply concrete success factors to unleash the energies and forces that today are still deep within your brand. Learning from winning brands is, we believe, the best way to create *new* winning brands.

2. *Linking any brand to a powerful purchase motive*: Today, many brands still seem to believe that all they need for growth is a powerful brand core. However, as strong and solid as it may be, they are consistently losing market share. That is because these brands lack the growth code that connects them to a compelling purchase motive. Cadillac is an example of an impressive brand core without a growth code. Marketing budgets are not for investing in a brand core, but for investing in the bottom line. Even brands that are built on image alone must be measured against its return.

3. *Systematically solving complex marketing problems*: Some marketing problems loom large and insurmountable – a huge competitor is steamrollering the market; consumers see your product as old-fashioned; your competitors are slashing prices. . . . The growth codes presented in this book point to sure-fire strategies for solving these problems systematically and effectively. In a sense, they work like a formula in mathematics – it will not solve the problem for you, but it makes the problem a lot easier to solve.

It is also an important merit of the growth codes that, again and again, they inspire creative and spectacularly successful solutions nobody ever thought of before. In Chapter 7, Working with growth codes, we will show you six examples of marketing problems that seem insurmountable and how the right growth code can lead to success.

## SUMMARY

Growth codes open new horizons. The experiences of the world's most successful brands are now something *tangible*. They can be accumulated, organized, differentiated, even combined. It is even possible to store this aggregate knowledge on a computer and access it via an expert system. Dialoguing with the system will define your problem and provide you with the strategic options for solving your specific marketing problem (cf. Chapter 8, Taking growth codes into the Internet age).

We now invite you to explore the five portals in the consumer's mind. We will enter them one by one and show you how any brand can become the logical choice.

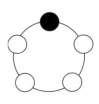

# Portal 1:
# Benefits &
# Promises

**Premise:** *Consumers prefer your brand because it offers a compelling (virtual) benefit.*

Deliver a unique product benefit and consumers will buy it. It can be that simple. But what if the quality of your product or service is just average? How does a brand grow without a tangible or apparent advantage over competitors? Before we look for answers, let us clarify quality. There are two sides to the coin: the *factual* quality, which refers to objective product benefits, i.e. materials, technology, even warranties, service points, etc; and the *virtual* quality, which is the consumer's *subjective* assessment. The reality is that brands with a high factual quality lose market share to those with a higher virtual quality.

To illustrate the point: a recent product survey showed that a certain generic facial creme was more effective in preventing wrinkles than most luxury brands on the market. By any objective standard, the luxury brands should have lost ground, while the low-priced brand's sales should have skyrocketed. However, consumers ignored the *facts* and instead *defended* the virtual superiority of the luxury brands. Is this a case *against* common sense? Not at all. It just points to the fact that, in most cases, buying a product or service means buying into a proposition, not a sum of objective benefits. Facts seem to play only a *supporting* role in the decision-making process, instead of driving it.

Here is an experiment: Picture a hundred typical household products that researchers have ranked on an objective quality scale. Now it is your turn to grade each product according to your subjective preference. We would not be surprised to find out that your subjective evaluation deviated from the "objective results" in more than 50% of the cases. But does this mean you were *wrong* 50% of the time? Does this mean we are all trapped in illusions? Of course not. How could all of us consumers be wrong all the time? We buy the products because *we feel like buying* them, not because they proved best in some high-tech laboratory.

## THERE IS NOTHING VIRTUAL ABOUT VIRTUAL QUALITY

Since the factual quality makes products and services interchangeable, our challenge is to create and sustain a *virtual* quality. Why does someone ask for a Bacardi instead of just rum? What is it that defines the gratification from drinking this particular brand? Of course, there is the pure flavor experience, a chemical reaction that involves taste buds and olfactory nerves – but it is not necessarily more rewarding than with other rums. There is more: say "Bacardi" and a movie unfolds in the mind, complete with Caribbean sunsets, sandy beaches, palm trees and the catchy beat of steel drums. This added value – developed, packaged and delivered by the brand – is an intrinsic part of the brand experience. Another brand might objectively taste the same, but if it does not come with a compelling experience in the mind, then the consumer is perfectly justified in saying ". . . but Bacardi tastes better." It tastes better because it delivers more.

## The Difference Virtual Quality Can Make

Consumers make a conscious choice for the *virtually* superior product, even if another product is *objectively* better. This point is illustrated by one battle in the never-ending cola wars: for a hundred years (from 1885 to 1985) Coca-Cola enjoyed the virtual advantage of being the Original ("The real thing") while Pepsi was the eternal runner-up. However, research disclosed that people preferred Pepsi to Coke whenever they were blindfolded in a test situation. This led to a worldwide campaign: "Take the Pepsi challenge!" Thousands of people were stopped in the street and were asked to rate Pepsi vs. Coke, with both labels covered. This way, Pepsi neutralized Coke's virtual edge and proved to be the superior product. The campaign rocked Coca-Cola's foundations at the worst moment: during Coke's centennial year. Executives were rattled to the extent that they no longer trusted in Coke's virtual superiority ("The Real Thing") and altered the formula. New Coke would be the better Pepsi and win back all those people who took the blindfold test. However, when Coke's pepsified cola hit the market, the move backfired in a public outcry, with picket lines and protests. From coast to coast, worried fans were stockpiling the old Coke in cellars and garden sheds. It did not matter to them that New Coke actually tasted better (more like Pepsi!) all they wanted was the "Original" back. Coca-Cola yielded to massive public pressure. They "reinstated" Coke Classic, combining contriteness with a renewed commitment to "The Real Thing." Ultimately, the brand not only regained lost territory, but also emerged stronger from the battle. What we learn from this is that *virtual* quality is more "real" to consumers than factual quality.

# THE GROWTH CODES FOR BENEFITS & PROMISES

It is in your brand's power to create a virtual edge. But where does it come from? Here are the five places to look.

1. *Addressing life interests*: How can your brand contribute towards fulfilling life interests, dreams and aspirations? The challenge is to move it up on the list of priorities in your consumer's life. *Get yourself on the agenda!* This approach can catapult even everyday products – be it milk, fabric softeners or even video games – from an *insignificant* to a *privileged* position in the consumer's mind.

2. *Pinpointing a threat*: Fears and anxieties come in many different shapes and sizes, from extra large to extra small. Your product or service can do a lot more than just solve a *problem* – it can be the silver bullet that eliminates a *fear*. If you thought insurance companies and alarm systems were the only candidates for this kind of strategy, then you will be surprised at the results it achieves for a cat litter, for instance, or an everyday kitchen product.

3. *Adopting a spirit*: Add a compelling virtual dimension to your brand by infusing it with a spirit – e.g. the *passion*, the *ambition*, the *attitude* or the *philosophy* of your company. This spirit melds with your brand and creates a *virtual* edge over *factually* comparable competitors. From breakfast cereals to computers to car rental companies – the spirit can be the key to new growth for just about any brand.

4. *Finding the magic*: Somewhere hidden in the core of your brand is some magic waiting to be discovered. Find it, define it and what you will give the consumer is something so fascinating, captivating and unique that your brand becomes the

logical choice. A soft drink, a cookie brand and a Belgian brewery experienced amazing brand growth with a little magic. So can your product or service.

5. *Making a mind-movie*: Make your brand the trigger of a stimulating, captivating mental film that automatically runs when somebody mentions your brand. With a mind-movie, your brand commands the center of the stage and makes your competitor the understudy.

All five approaches are based on universal growth codes that can be systematically applied to the most diverse products and services. They are not formulas for churning out standard strategies. Instead, they point at ways of creating a virtual quality you may never have thought possible.

## 1. Addressing Life Interests

What part does your product play in the consumer's life? Let us be honest: most consumption products, measured against the consumer's life interests appear *hopelessly insignificant*. How crucial is a fabric softener, a paper towel or baked beans compared with those issues that *really* count? Feeling good, a happy family, good friends, a rewarding career, fulfilling hobbies, holidays, prosperity, health and security are just some of the important issues that occupy our minds 95% of the time. All those thousands of products and services out there are competing for the remaining 5%.

The challenge for your brand is to make the leap from relative insignificance onto your consumer's exclusive *agenda of life interests*. What if your brand could actively contribute toward fulfilling or achieving those needs and goals we just mentioned? Take a fabric softener, for instance, that for years had been positioned with the promise of "downy softness". Ask the consumer where downy soft towels rank on his or her agenda of important things in life and the answer will probably be somewhere around position 1365. But what is to keep us from moving up the agenda? Somewhere close to the top we arrive at a completely new proposition: *feeling comfortable after a hard day's work.* Ask where that ranks in importance, and you are talking Top 10. Here is a life interest our fabric softener can truly help fulfill.

Keep in mind that your consumer's agenda is not just filled with big visions, high aspirations and dreams, however. We have just seen how important the *small* things are – those precious moments that make us happy and feel fulfilled every day: enjoying a little peace and quiet on your own; kudos from your colleagues after making an impressive presentation; or savoring a great accomplishment. In short, the small things that make your day. *Contributing* to these natural highs or even boosting them is what gets your brand on the consumer's agenda.

Remember this: it is not enough simply associating your brand with the consumer's life interests – you have to make them happen!

## The Agenda Principle

*Look at your consumer's life interests and determine how your brand can contribute toward fulfilling them. Get on the consumers agenda!*

Success factors:

1. *Link*: The new role you are defining for your brand must be directly related to a *basic benefit* of your product or service. The clearer the relationship between *product* benefit and *life* benefit, the better. Example: a men's fragrance may by virtue of its product benefit ("pleasant fragrance") address an important life benefit in the male mind ("increase

sex appeal"). However, it is rather doubtful that a great-tasting, easy-to-spread margarine can be the cause of family harmony and happiness at the breakfast table. If the link is tenuous, you will lose the consumer's attention.

2. *Focus*: Address a *specific* life interest. Correlate your brand with a *specific situation* in which this interest is met or fulfilled. It is not enough for, say, a vitamin booster to just promise "more oomph". Identify key moments in the consumer's life when performance sags and an energy boost would make all the difference. Secondly, it is very important to give a clear picture of the *degree* to which the consumer's performance, alertness, etc. increases.

3. *Competition*: The Agenda Principle works best when your competition is primarily selling on practical quality and performance attributes. This is your opportunity to make your brand part of the big picture of a consumer's agenda of life interests.

The following examples illustrate how the Agenda Principle can grow products and services into winning brands. The Norwegian Cruise Line, once a leader in the vacation cruise market, saw bookings decline over the years. It seemed nothing could stem the downward trend . . .

## Case in point: Norwegian Cruise Line (USA)

Norwegian Cruise Line (NCL) sales were declining rapidly as a result of aggressive pricing within the industry and increasing competition from other types of holiday and tour operators. The situation was bad and getting worse. Cruise operators all basically offered the same thing: showgirls, shuffleboard and mountains of food. There were no compelling factual selling points going for the NCL. What should they do? Let us look at it from a life agenda perspective: now, it becomes clear that cruises in general rank pretty low on most peoples agenda, because they are expensive compared with most other kinds of holidays. So, how can NCL move up on the agenda? The idea is to address the ulterior *life interest* behind the usual commodities of a cruise. What do consumers *really* want from a vacation? *They want to be liberated from the frustrating limitations of their everyday lives – they want to escape!* This is where NCL, by its own nature as a cruise line, can link up with an important life interest that catapults it out of their competitive environment.

The new proposition: "The laws of the land do not apply." On NCL cruise ships, for instance, there is "no law that says you cannot make love at four o'clock in the afternoon on a Tuesday". Get away from it all and leave all those tedious conventions, rules and regulations far behind! Here is a compelling purchase motive that struck a chord with consumers to the point that NCL cruises were subsequently booked solid for every trip. Let us keep in mind that NCL did not change the factual quality of its services in any way. Instead, it created a compelling virtual edge that clicked with the consumers.

The State of Illinois Tourism Board is another example of addressing the consumer's agenda of life interests. By putting itself "a million miles from Monday," the Land of Lincoln did not choose the conventional route of praising landscapes and landmarks – where it was at a disadvantage compared with neighboring states. Instead, it captured the essence of what a getaway weekend is all about.

Let us now have a look at everyday products. How can they facilitate the achievement of a lifetime goal? Here is how the Agenda Principle worked for milk in the United Kingdom to overcome a seemingly hopeless market situation:

## Case in point: Milk (United Kingdom)

Per capita milk consumption had dropped 30% and the British Dairy Association was becoming very concerned indeed. How do we stop the trend? Can it be stopped, let alone reversed? In the primary youth market, soft drinks were chugging away share of throat and it seemed nothing could be done about it. The obvious arguments – milk is fresh, milk energizes, milk tastes good – seemed weak, worn and boring. And obviously "fresh, energizing and great-tasting milk" is not a high priority on a child's agenda of life interests.

How can we move it up? Is it a stretch to believe that drinking milk in your childhood is one of the reasons you will grow big and strong? One simple truth seemed to have been forgotten along the way: "Milk is good for the physical development of children". Or, in kids' words: "If you want to grow up to be a great athlete, you'd better drink milk." This is our powerful new proposition. Becoming a great athlete one day is something every kid dreams of. It is way up on the agenda.

One of the TV advertisements showed two kids chatting after sports. One drinks lemonade, the other chooses milk, which the lemonade fan cannot understand. "Milk?! Ugh!" The young milk fan counters that Ian Rush (a famous athlete) recommends milk and concludes: "Don't drink milk, then. You'll just end up playing for Accrington Stanley." – "Accrington Stanley? Who are they?" – "Exactly," is the laconic answer.

The market rewarded this with a 12% increase in milk consumption within the 2–8-year-old age group. Not only was the strategy a huge success in increasing milk sales, but the "exactly" also entered the vernacular of schoolyards across the United Kingdom.

The Agenda Principle is a proven strategy for putting products and services of virtually any industry on a track to strong growth. Unlock its potential for your brand by drawing up an agenda of life interests from your consumer's perspective:

- What are the goals, plans, desires and ideals for improving his or her life situation for the short, mid and long term – where does your brand fit in?
- What are the situations, big or small, that bring happiness or contentment in a life or at a specific stage in life – how does your brand relate to them?
- What are the major obstacles in the way of achieving these goals – how could your brand remove them?

These are just some ways of looking at your consumer's priorities and identifying the possibilities of propelling your brand from a position of *relative insignificance* to one of *major significance*. It is a chance to perceive your brand as part of a broader context that reaches far beyond *factual* benefits. Mapping your brand against the consumer's agenda will point to opportunities that, so far, may never have crossed your mind.

## 2. Pinpointing a Threat

The opposite of the big and small things that make our day are the fears that can ruin it. Some loom large, like losing our job, falling ill, or a bad accident. Others are small, everyday fears and concerns that accompany us during our daily lives, like wrinkles, zits and being overweight, or not living up to expectations at the workplace – or in bed. We buy a bathtub mat for fear of slipping and breaking our neck in the shower. And we always have an umbrella handy in case it rains. Whether it is the fear of offending someone with our bad breath or the threat of a hurricane if you live in a tropical storm area, fears are very powerful forces that motivate actions – and purchases.

Of course, "fear-fighting" is an obvious strategy for an insurance policy, an alarm system or even a mouthwash. However, even *the most unlikely* brands can achieve outstanding growth by pinpointing – and eliminating – a threat that consumers had not registered before. The idea is to turn your thinking around. Do not ask, "What's in it for the consumer?" but "What is the fear I am putting to rest with my brand?" Pinpoint a (long-term) threat that lurks behind *not using* your product. Here is the growth code . . .

---

### The Risk Principle

*Pinpoint a (long-term) risk or threat in your consumer's life and position your brand as the ideal means of eliminating it.*

Success factors:

1. *Intensity*: Does the risk or threat you are pointing at really worry your consumers? If the risk is negligible, they will shrug at it. If it is overwhelming, they will deny it.

2. *Probability*: Check the odds of the risk as perceived by the consumer. Make sure the statistics are on your side. Make a case for how *omnipresent* the risk is in everyday life.

3. *Competence*: Consumers must perceive your brand as an effective means to eliminate the fear. Otherwise, as research shows, the strategy will backfire.

There are plenty of brands out there that push a fear button, of course, but they push the one that is already glowing bright red. Your brand can put fears to rest that consumers may never have associated with your brand. The following case shows how even the most unlikely brands can pinpoint a threat that makes buying it a "must."

## Case in point: Tidy Cat (USA)

Tidy Cat is a cat litter that eliminates pesky odors, not more or less effectively than any other brand. Increasing competition was threatening Tidy Cat's franchise. What was the way out of this deteriorating market situation? Tidy Cat looked *beyond* the problem of pesky odors and considered what fear it could put to rest. This led to a completely new positioning: "Tidy Cat is the cat litter that protects you from embarrassment in front of your guests." Here was a real, understandable social risk that rang a louder alarm bell than unpleasant odors.

The commercial takes us to a dinner party in a posh home. Suddenly, one of the guests twitches his nostrils – what on earth is this smell?! He sniffs again, raises his eyebrow and flares his nostrils. The pungent smell just will not go away. Finally, the man leans over to the hostess and carefully whispers: "Do I smell . . . *pie*?" And she is absolutely mortified. The tag-line explains it all: "If it's anything less than Tidy Cat, you'll know."

We have just seen how the Risk Principle can be applied to link your brand to an existing fear in the consumers' mind, thus establishing a powerful new purchase motive. Let us now turn to the second growth code for pinpointing a threat: the Villain Principle. This one applies if your brand is fighting a problem that seems vague, abstract or insignificant to the consumer. You can make that problem tangible, give it an ominous name and an ugly face! Make it a villain that is a real threat to your consumers. They do not have any choice but to fight it!

How to create a villain is something we can learn from politics. Pollution, for instance, had been a concern for years but to many people it was a rather abstract problem, one out of hundreds. Then the term "acid rain" was coined and this bad name turned the vague problem into a dangerous villain. Suddenly, people felt threatened and the topic became a hot item in the mass media. The person on the street could hardly assess the scope of the damage to our forests, but "acid rain" conjured up a terrible vision of decimated forests and withering trees that no longer generated the air we need to breathe. It motivated entire populations to alter their behavior. Acid rain became a villain we were determined to fight.

Now, how do you make your brand a "weapon" to fight a villain that your consumers have not yet been aware of? Here is the growth code.

---

### The Villain Principle

*Turn the problem your brand solves into a villain – give him an ominous name and an ugly face. Position your brand as the silver bullet.*

Success factors:

1. *Fear potential*: The new villain must be threatening enough to motivate action against him. This depends on the name and the face you give him – is he *bad* enough? Find out how intense consumer reactions are to this new threat. Important: objectively, the threat has always been there, but now you are making the consumer aware of it.

2. *Credibility*: The consumer *must* perceive your product as the most effective means of combating the villain. Also: the name, color and or shape of your product go a long way towards reinforcing perceived effectiveness – and credibility.

The following case study shows how a freezer bag brand turned a seemingly irrelevant problem into the villain number one in German kitchens – and jump-started sales. . . .

## Case in point: Melitta Toppits (Germany–Europe)

Cheaper brands and generic products were eroding Melitta Toppits' market share; within just a few years it had dropped 13%. Even if Melitta Toppits was objectively a better product, why should consumers pay extra for a brand when any little plastic bag will obviously do the job? The clock was ticking.

The strategic leap was to look at the product from a new angle: Yes, we know that Melitta Toppits preserves food in the freezer – but *against* what? Who is the villain? The only thing that emerges here is the threat of ruptured bags. A vague risk, one that is hardly noticeable – nothing to get excited about. Again, who's the villain? "Melitta Toppits protects your food against 'Freezer Burn'." That is the ominous name for our villain. Now picture the frightening image of frosted food sticking out of burst bags that not only looks disgusting but has also lost some of its nutritious value.

The brand transformed an insignificant issue into a bona fide threat that homemakers could not possibly ignore or tolerate. As a result of positioning itself as the silver bullet against a horrible villain, Melitta Toppits not only stemmed the decline in sales, but also achieved a 42% increase within three years.

Pinpointing a threat can inspire surprisingly effective strategies for products and services you would normally never picture in a "fear context."

## 3. Adopting a Spirit

Picture a pair of elegant brand name shoes. They appear perfect in every respect: design, leather grade, finish, color and wear comfort. The quality of the materials and the precision of the processes justify the premium price. And yet, given the choice, the consumer will feel more attracted to a *hand-sewn* pair from a small, exclusive shoemaker. What does the second pair have that the first one does not? Surely, a machine designed for maximum precision will do a better job at sewing together a shoe than our shoemaker. But it is the shoemaker's passion, his ambition, his personal care that adds value to the hand-sewn shoes. Here, we touch upon the *spirit* that infuses the product with an extra dimension of quality. It is a virtual quality that not even the best machines in the world can match.

It is the same thing with grandma's strawberry preserve: it simply tastes better than the stuff in the jar from the supermarket. Why? Because it's *made with love*. Would grandma's jam stand a chance against branded mass products in a blindfold test? Maybe not. Whether it is shoes or marmalade, the spirit behind your brand adds a virtual quality that is hard to beat.

Adopting a spirit is about defining the *quality* of your product or service as a *result* of what *you* believe in. It can be expressed as

- an *ambition* – e.g. a department store: "Good is not good enough for us."
- an *attitude* – e.g. a financial services company: "We make money the old-fashioned way. We earn it," or

- a *philosophy* – e.g. a baby food manufacturer that proclaims a ecological mission.

What is the right spirit for your brand? Ask yourself what kind of spirit it takes to achieve *excellence* in your product or service category. If your company makes baby food, one spirit behind excellent baby food could be a "back to nature" philosophy. Consumers will consider your products to be more *natural* than the competition, and thus have a higher quality. This is now your virtual edge.

Now think of a computer company. What is the spirit behind excellence in this business? To Apple it is the spirit of innovation. Its "Think different" attitude makes bold, unconventional thinking a prerequisite for cutting edge technology. Now think of a bourbon brand. What drives excellence here? An *innovative* spirit? Certainly not. The best bourbon is the kind that is made the old-fashioned way – you want the bourbon to be infused with a *traditional* spirit. Because *traditional* is what adds the virtual quality.

The key to making your new spirit a powerful engine for growth is to *polarize* your own "right" spirit against the "wrong" spirit of the rest of the market. Here are three examples.

1. British carrier Virgin Atlantic exposes the "wrong" attitude of competitive airlines by parodying flight attendant stereotypes – the fashion model, the drill sergeant, the flirt – while showing Virgin's flight attendants as truly wanting to be flight attendants (the "right" attitude).

2. Car rental company Avis, then the number two in the market, put the onus on Hertz, the eternal number one, by vocalizing their "We try harder" philosophy – harder than Hertz, is what is implied. And that is quite plausible, too: it makes sense

that the number two is motivated to go the extra mile in serving its customers (the "right" spirit). And it makes just as
much sense to assume that the eternal number one is getting
complacent and has lost the "gleam" in its eyes (the "wrong"
spirit).

3. The Washington Mutual Savings Bank, a local bank in the
   United States, had to defend its turf against big national
   players that offered all the state-of-the-art commodities,
   opportunities and service packages. Here, the big idea was to
   polarize: The spirit of the big competitors who do not really
   care about the region and the people living there (the "wrong"
   spirit) against the spirit of Washington Mutual Savings Bank
   that keeps offering friendly and personal service (the "right"
   spirit).

How the Spirit Principle works:

---

## The Spirit Principle

*Add a spirit to your brand that implies superior quality
(the "right" spirit) and polarizes your competitors (the
"wrong" spirit).*

Success factors:

1. *Relevance*: The consumers must be able to translate
   the spirit you are adopting directly into a quality
   expectation. How *relevant* is your spirit to making
   *superior* products or services?

2. *Credibility*: Adopting a spirit is not about putting on
   a new label – you must be able to live up to it. If you
   can't make it, don't fake it.

3. *Repositioning competitors*: The clearer you oppose your "right" spirit to the "wrong" spirit of the rest of the market, the stronger your position.

4. *Simplicity:* Capture the spirit of your company in just one thought. Do not make it a manifesto.

The following example illustrates in greater detail how adding a spirit translates into brand growth.

## Case in point: Post Waffle Crisp (USA)

When Post Waffle Crisps, part of Kraft General Foods, was introduced, achieving a 0.5% market share was considered a lofty goal. In a market where brand loyalty is high and products cannot be differentiated in terms of quality, this mission was quite a challenge.

Compounding the problem was the fact that sweetened, ready-to-eat cereals suffer from a bad reputation as industrialized "fast food." What could the Post Waffle Crisp people do about it? There was no point in changing the ingredients. But they could add something new that would catapult them out of their competitive environment: the right spirit. "Post Waffle Crisps are made with love." Loving care is the way you remember breakfast as a kid and it is the way you want your kids to experience breakfast. That is a compelling purchase motive. What made the new strategy all the more powerful was the fact that consumers now assumed that the competitor's products were "made without love" – namely, by industrial machines. No heart and no soul, there.

How does the "spirit" strategy come alive? One commercial shows a quaint little Post Waffle Crisp factory in which an army of charming grannies are happily baking Post Waffle Crisps with minuscule waffle irons, individually and by hand. Everything about this picture spells tender loving care in making a healthy breakfast cereal. It creates a virtual added value that captures the consumer's imagination and amplifies the growth potential. Post Waffle Crisp exceeded all projections within the first year of its introduction.

How would you define the spirit behind your brand in a nutshell? How would *consumers* perceive it? Would it translate into a virtual positive or into a virtual negative? And what about your competitors? Does a positive, iron-clad spirit back their product or service? Or is there a chink in the armor that your brand can prize open?

## 4. Finding the Magic

One of the most precious virtual qualities a brand can possess is magic. Do not be too quick to answer that your product has none. We will look at everyday products that have grown into national and international successes on the strength of the magic that was discovered within them – a soft drink, a sore throat drop and a cookie brand are just a few examples. Obviously, magic is not a tangible characteristic of your product: it lies deep in the brand core. It is much like looking at a pebble and then discovering through a magnifying glass that it is a raw diamond.

But what exactly is magic? We define it as an *intriguing implausibility* that is attached to a product or service. It is a special something that cannot be (fully) explained with our logic, our experience and our knowledge of the world. Most of us lead such an orderly, explainable, familiar life – we know all its possibilities and limitations. And all we do not know science can certainly explain in a rational and plausible way. And that is exactly why we find it so intriguing to walk the thin line between the plausible and the implausible – by letting some magic into our world. Magic challenges our reason, captures our imagination and will simply not leave us alone. Imagine how a little magic can set your brand apart from the competition, which suddenly looks rather boring.

---

### The Magic Principle

*Capture the "intriguing implausibility" within your brand that makes your competitors look boring.*

Success factors:

1. *Fascination*: The "intriguing implausibility" must not only clearly differentiate your brand from competitors, but also rise above their *factual* selling points. Confirm your competitive edge with consumers.

2. *Credibility*: Define how the magic got into your brand. Is there a special ingredient at work? Or are there other indicators of magic – an exotic origin, unusual aesthetics, a foreign name, etc?

---

The following case studies demonstrate how magic can be brought to the surface and how their "intriguing implausibility" became a bankable asset. The first case looks at a completely new kind of beverage, the pioneer of so-called energy drinks. . . .

---

### Case in point: Red Bull (Germany)

Red Bull has its roots in Southeast Asia and was the first energy drink in Europe. It wakes you up the way several cups of coffee do, but you will not feel as wired. The taste is special, too, rather like a fizzy cough syrup. It comes from a stimulant called Taurin, which is similar to caffeine. But what are we marketing here? A coffee substitute with a strange taste and a funny name? Not surprisingly, some renowned research company strongly advised against the launch of this drink. A difficult situation. How do you make Red Bull a staggering success? The marketing people delved deeper into the brand and searched for the magic hidden inside. As a starting point, the strange overall appeal of the new brand is a fertile soil for magic: the remote origin, the little-known stimulant, the name, the taste. The challenge was to capture the intriguing implausibility that sets Red Bull worlds apart from coffee and other beverages.

Here is the magical proposition: "Red Bull gives you wings." This challenges the imagination of consumers: What might this exciting new experience feel like? People got hooked on the magic – it became a powerful purchase motive. Even in its fourth year, Red Bull was growing at 42% and had four to five times more market share than its next best competitor. This despite countless new energy drinks jumping on the bandwagon.

But how do you make this magic understandable in a creative message to the consumer? A series of commercials shows us cartoon characters caught in precarious situations and how Red Bull saves the day by making them sprout wings. In one spot, for instance, we see two missionaries simmering in a huge black cauldron and waiting to be served to cannibals. The situation seems hopeless until one of them pulls out a can of Red Bull. No sooner do both take a gulp than our two missionaries sprout wings and simply flutter out of the soup.

This is not to say that only particularly exotic products have the monopoly on magic. Magic can be a credible approach even for the most conventional item – like medication against a sore throat.

## Case in point: Hall's Soothers (United Kingdom)

When Hall's introduced its new Soothers, the new medication looked just like any other cough drop. It blended a reliable efficacy with a pretty good taste. But is that enough to lead the brand to a staggering success? Probably not. To find a powerful strategy we need to get deeper into the product. We discover that Hall's Soothers indeed create a different feeling in the throat. They do not give you that biting and then numbing feeling so characteristic of other drops or throat lozenges. This new feeling is hard to define and is certainly not related to the efficacy of the product. However, what we have here is the seed of an intriguing implausibility: Hall's Soothers are *kissing* it better. The complete disconnect between the well-known experience of sucking on a cough drop and Hall's proposition is what captures the imagination – combined with the allusion to getting kissed where it hurts. Just imagine you are in a drugstore aisle rubbing your sore throat as you stand in front of a shelf with throat and cough drops. Which one would you choose? The kind that works and tastes good? Or the kind that will kiss it better? It is the intriguing implausibility here that determines your choice. Hall's Soothers exceeded their projections by more than double the share to 12% in just 1.5 years after product launch.

As we have seen, the *magical action* of a product can be a specific physical feeling, like a kiss from Hall's Soothers. Many brands are very successful because they trigger an intriguingly implausible *reaction* on the part of the consumer. Here are three examples.

1. In the United States, Baskin–Robbins's Chocolate Blast promised to make anybody who tried it an instant "chocoholic." It is the "addictive" component that

separates this brand from all other competitive ice creams.

2. Savoring Walker's Crisps, a British potato chip, invariably leads to a complete loss of self-control. Even the nicest guys turn into loony fanatics after the first chip touches their lips. Of course, consumers are burning to find out what makes this brand so different.

3. Stella Artois, a premium Belgian beer, drives people to make unbelievable *sacrifices* just for a pint of Stella. A hard day of work repairing the roof of a pub in the province is one example of what people are willing to do just to afford one glass of this "reassuringly expensive" lager.

As long as there will be brands, magic will remain a compelling way to win consumers. It is all the more powerful in mundane, everyday products. The challenge is to look beyond the conventional in your brand and find that *intriguing implausibility*.

## 5. Making a Mind-Movie

Envision the mind of the consumer as being a huge audio-visual archive. As soon as you hear a specific word, your mind's eye conjures up a picture, a series of pictures, perhaps even sounds and smells. Take "New York," for instance. Close your eyes and what happens? Instantly a small mind-movie starts running, feeding back your personal associations with New York: Times Square, the skyline, Broadway, Central Park, horse carriages, Wall Street, bustling sidewalks, police sirens and fire engines. . . .

From the French Revolution to the Kosovo Conflict, from Bill Clinton to Monica Lewinski, from Greenland to Fiji, from Stone Age to Universe – almost every term you know will evoke a little mind-movie that blends your personal experiences with images you have seen, information you have read and stories you have heard. The quality and length of the movie varies, of course: some movies are just a jumble of images, while others arrange themselves into a logical sequence. Some are out of focus and jarred, while others are sharp, alive and full of color, smells and sounds.

The following example illustrates how a mind-movie can impact the purchase decision process. Imagine you are in an antique shop, looking at two cabinets. The first one is very ornate, with intricate decorations and it is in perfect condition. It is a beautiful piece of furniture, you agree, as the dealer points out all the details that make up its flawless quality. The second one is not as intricately designed and has a few, hardly noticeable, flaws – but this one comes with a history. The dealer does not focus on detail and workmanship, but instead waxes poetic. Ah, this cabinet is from a castle in France that belonged to a nobleman who was a secret emissary to the English court during the French Revolution. Which cabinet would you buy? Chances are you would choose the second one because it engages a mind-movie of fascinating images: you imagine a castle in France, a family hiding during the French Revolution, secret letters hidden in a drawer, the cabinet collecting dust over the centuries. . . . Compared with this "history" the first cabinet loses some of its luster and becomes just another useful, albeit beautiful, piece of furniture. It goes to show how the mind-movie creates and defines a virtual added value that can be decisive for the purchase decision. It also shows that shortcomings in terms of factual quality can easily be compensated by a stronger, virtual added value.

How do brand professionals direct compelling mind-movies? Where do they start? A case study cited by management consultants Jack Trout and Al Ries, gives us a good track to run on. The assignment was to boost American tourist travel to Jamaica, at the time a relatively unknown Caribbean holiday destination.

Although Jamaica offered a host of attractions, to most Americans it was just another banana republic. The solution lay in taking a classic mind-movie ("Hawaii") and changing its title, as it were, to Jamaica – as in "Jamaica is Hawaii in the Caribbean." This new positioning caused all the associations conjured up by Hawaii – a whole package of images, experiences and expectations – to be transferred to Jamaica. The fact that it was new, closer, less expensive and had the same sandy beaches, sunshine days per year, mountains and leafy valleys made Jamaica all the more attractive. Instead of building a new positioning from scratch at the cost of considerable time and money, Jamaica was surfing on a huge wave generated by Hawaii.

On the practical side, how do you know what the right mind-movie might be for your brand? How do you know whether it will work and lead your brand to new growth? For one thing, the mind-movie must project *specific values* onto your brand that are *relevant to the consumer's purchase decision* – as we saw in the case of Jamaica.

To illustrate this process, let us look at Finlandia, a Finnish vodka that owes its success on the US market to a compelling mind-movie. The challenge was to establish this small European brand as a new alternative to Russian and Swedish vodkas – against overwhelming odds. The process of developing an effective mind-movie can be broken down into three steps:

1. *Define the most important brand values for the purchase decision*: Put down on paper exactly what expectations your consumer has of the *ideal* product or service. An ideal vodka, for instance (a) comes from Russia, (b) is clear and pure (c) is ice cold. How does Finlandia deliver on these points? Obviously, we cannot compete with a Russian origin, but we can work on the "clean and pure" and the "ice cold" part.

2. *Find the mind-movie that fits*: What associations does the consumer's mind make with "clean and pure" and "ice cold"? Is there a mind-movie we can use? Search for it in your brand environment: where does it comes from, how is it made, what is it called, who uses it?. . . Our Finnish vodka comes with a built-in solution: the keyword "Finland" in itself generates a little mind-movie that fits in relatively well with the values of "clean" and "pure." And "ice cold" is readily associated with Finland's arctic geography.

3. *Edit the mind-movie*: The "Finland" mind-movie as it stands now is still disjointed, out of focus: images of landscapes, people and animals come to mind; but also political, economic or social themes may appear. We need to sort things out and focus on what is relevant to the values of "cold, clean and pure." Cutting through the clutter brings our mind-movie into focus: "Vodka from the top of the world." Finlandia is now part of the arctic world, a barren but pristine expanse of crystal clear ice, blinding sunshine, biting cold and pure winter air. No people, no cities, no forests and no elks. The "Finland" mind-movie now drives home only what is relevant to the brand: "cold, clean and pure."

The strategy paid off for Finlandia and it is still successfully standing its ground against much bigger vodka brands. More important, Finlandia has achieved much more than other vodka brands that also claim to be "cold, clean and pure." The mind-movie melds these three values into a powerful, compelling proposition that is now credibly synonymous with "Finlandia." In order to beat Finlandia, a competitor would first have to direct a more powerful, more compelling mind-movie.

To summarize these conclusions into a workable growth code:

---

**The Mind-Movie Principle**

*Link your brand to a mind-movie that projects those specific values which are relevant to the purchase decision.*

Success factors:

1. *Link*: The mind-movie must build on brand or product values – origin, ingredients, color, shape or even the way it is used . . .

2. *Relevance*: The brand values you project must be relevant to the purchase decision. What are the *ideal* values your consumer expects?

3. *Fascination*: The mind-movie must capture the consumer's imagination. It is not just *descriptive.* How sharp, evocative and intriguing are the images? The more exciting and fascinating they are, the more value you add to your product.

---

Put your product or service to the test by closing your eyes and switching the projector on: is a mind-movie running? If so, what are the values, images your brand conjures up? Is the mind-movie compelling enough to become the purchase motive? Or could there be a different mind-movie that might give your product or service an even stronger, more unique virtual value?

## SUMMARY

We have now crossed the Benefits & Promises portal and familiarized ourselves with a choice of five universal growth codes.

Each is focused on creating or enhancing the virtual quality of your product or service in such a manner that it makes your brand the logical choice:

- Addressing life interests catapults your brand out of relative insignificance onto the consumer's agenda of important needs and goals.

- Pinpointing a threat shows how even the most everyday products help us by checking off one more item on the list of things we find ourselves worrying about.

- Adopting a spirit is about infusing your brand with an ambition, an attitude or a philosophy that leverages its virtual quality.

- Finding the magic means uncovering an "intriguing implausibility" beneath the surface of your brand.

- Projecting a mind-movie makes your brand the trigger of vivid mental images that enhance the brand experience.

Remember, the growth codes we have defined for each approach are universal and applicable to all diverse industries, target groups, cultures. As we move on to the remaining four portals, we will explore psychological and emotional purchase motives, which have nothing to do with benefits and quality at all. Aha, you are thinking, now we are talking soft selling. Not true: we will present a number of sure-fire growth codes that will radically remap the market to your advantage.

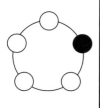 # Portal 2: Norms & Values

**Premise:** *Consumers prefer your brand because it solves or avoids an inner conflict (with their norms and values).*

Norms and values motivate human actions – and thus purchase behavior – just as effectively as an attractive (virtual) benefit. Values, of course, cover the sum of all ethical, moral and social orientations in our mind – our sense of duty, loyalty, fairness, propriety, etc. These abstract values translate into concrete norms that effectively dictate our behavior from morning to night. The alarm clock goes off in the morning and already the first orders are issued: Time to get up! – Brush your teeth! – Put on a tie! – Take the garbage on the way out! – Don't be late! . . . And so on throughout the day. Disobeying or rebelling against these norms is not easy; whenever we do, we feel an inner sting.

Norms and values, then, sharply contrast with Benefits & Promises. "What's in it for me?" is not the question here, but rather, "What is the right thing to do?" Every choice we make is automatically checked against moral, ethical and social norms that either support or reject it. The benefits we want and the norms we abide by are two opposing forces that are constantly competing against each other. Should I go to the swimming pool on Saturday (benefit) or should I keep my promise (norm) to help my friend with moving to the new apartment? Should I leave this boring party (benefit) or should I be polite (norm) and hang in there another hour? Should I have the fling (benefit) or should I be faithful (norm) to my companion? Every disinterested action we take, every choice to let an irresistible opportunity go by, is almost always the result of moral commands that override the gratification from an immediate benefit.

## HOW NORMS AND VALUES RULE OUR EVERYDAY LIVES

Think about how often moral, ethical or social considerations make you do one thing instead of another. You might even be surprised at how strongly the course of your day is dictated by norms and values. Think of your sense of . . .

- Duty
- Responsibility
- Pride
- Honor
- Courtesy
- Decency
- Shame
- Generosity
- Fairness
- Gratitude
- Loyalty
- Compassion

And these are just some of the powerful motivators behind our actions. The interesting thing is that we do not act out of any of the above reasons because we see a benefit coming our way, but because we *must*. They constitute our *value system*, telling us what is the right thing to do at any given moment.

## THE AMAZING POWER OF NORMS AND VALUES

The hold of moral, ethical or social values on our minds is demonstrated in *extreme* cases: individuals will disregard substantial personal advantages only to satisfy their moral norms. They will also make amazing sacrifices in order to live up to their value system and keep it intact. *The Guinness Book of Records* has an entry for the most honest man alive: Lowell Elliott, a farmer from Indiana, once found a suitcase on his property that contained US$500000. There were no eyewitnesses; nobody would have been the wiser if he had taken the money and retired to Hawaii. Lowell Elliott gave the money to the police, every last cent of it. Should he have kept the money (benefit) or see that it was returned to its rightful owner (norm)? Elliott's value system was so solid that there was no choice at all.

Hollywood once took the conflict between benefits and norms to a shocking height with the film *Indecent Proposal*. Here, aging billionaire John Cage offers a young and attractive real estate agent a million dollars in exchange for spending one night with him. She is married and the couple are in dire financial straits. Is a million dollars a big enough benefit to override a sacred norm ("I should not prostitute myself.")? The film sparked a major debate on morality in the United States and everywhere it was shown in the world. To many, there was and is no price high enough to justify breaking the norm.

Norms can also be ruthless, as a psychological experiment in the United States with a shocking outcome proved. "Scientists" visited a class of 13 to 14 year olds and asked for volunteers for an *important scientific test* of hearing sensitivity. There was one caveat, the important-looking men in their white coats candidly admitted: the risk of a 50% hearing loss. Out of the 42 pupils, 39 volunteered to operate a so-called "Sound Generator" and send a special, high-frequency noise signal of gradually increasing intensity into their headset. Each volunteer could observe the danger level increasing inexorably on a large display from 0 (no danger of hearing loss) to 8 (50% hearing loss) – with a red arc until 10 (total and permanent hearing loss!) At all times, a scientist was right next to the pupil, there to assist and in a neutral voice explain the importance of this experiment.

Of the pupils, 70% dutifully complied with all the instructions and voluntarily risked losing 50% of their hearing. The signal was fake, of course, so no volunteer was ever at risk. The experiment proves the power of a norm. The sense of duty ("It is your duty to assist science and obey the scientist!") was stronger than any instinct of self-preservation.

Ethical, moral or social norms and values can be so strong that individuals will die for them. A true account of the *Titanic* disaster relates of four billionaires on the *Titanic* who readily ceded their seats on one of the lifeboats to women and children, but perfect strangers all the same. "Women and children first!" was a norm so deeply ingrained in these four gentlemen that they voluntarily sacrificed a chance to save themselves.

## HOW NORMS CAN BE USED TO ALTER HUMAN BEHAVIOR

By now we should be able to agree that norms have an extraordinary influence on human behavior. But you might also be tempted to believe that all these motivations only come from *within* – and cannot be impacted by an external influence. That is not the case. Norms can be defined and applied from *outside* as well. Psychologists, for instance, use new norms as effective tools for altering behavioral patterns and helping individuals with serious personality disorders. The following example from modern psychiatry tells of a 16-year-old girl who could not keep from sucking her thumb. Neither rational arguments nor punishments from her parents, nor even the jeering she suffered in school, could break the habit. That is, until Milton H. Erickson, one of the leading psychiatrists of the time, devised the following therapy: the girl was *instructed* to suck her thumb at a set time each day and for a set period. Within a few days the teenager kicked the habit. What Erickson did was to redefine *rebellious behavior* ("sucking your thumb") into an *conformism*. The girl's desire to *break* a norm had become the religious *fulfillment* of a norm – there suddenly was no point in sucking her thumb anymore. This form of therapy is called paradoxical intervention. It is just one way of using norms as an external means of altering behavioral patterns into a certain direction.

## HOW NORMS AND VALUES INFLUENCE PURCHASE DECISIONS

Norms can be the feather that tips the scale for or against buying a specific brand. Here are a few examples:

- Millions of consumers now prefer environmentally friendly products. In the case of detergents, for instance, choice has less to do with the cleansing benefit and more with fulfilling a *societal norm*; namely, preserving the environment.

- Consumers will even boycott a brand if it goes against their norms and values. *Benetton*, for instance, shocked the public with advertising that depicted a bleeding soldier, a dying Aids patient, etc. The campaign went so strongly against prevalent norms of decency that 100 franchises in Germany had to declare bankruptcy.

But there are other, perhaps less "morally charged" norms that are no less effective in dictating our buying patterns. The psychological price barrier is one example. There are a number of commodity products that are up against a *price* norm: a half pound of butter must not cost more than 95 cents. A brand priced at just US$1.05 will have a tougher time, even though the extra dime is not going to hurt anybody's pocketbook. It is about a set norm that makes refusing to pay more than 95 cents a matter of principle.

To summarize: norms and values will often motivate human behavior more effectively than the reward of a personal benefit. However strong they may be, norms can be replaced by other, stronger norms to alter behavior.

## THE GROWTH CODES FOR NORMS & VALUES

The stage is now set for exploring the ways in which this knowledge of norms, values and their impact on human behavior translates into sure-fire strategies for brand growth. Beyond the Norms & Values portal we find four distinctive approaches.

1. *Eliminating guilt*: Forgetting a wedding anniversary, not spending enough time with the kids, not having been in touch with so and so in ages. . . . These are just some of the failings that sting and gnaw at our conscience. The ability to eliminate such feelings of guilt is a unique strength that brands can capitalize on. Products as diverse as a kids' lunch and a greeting card illustrate the effectiveness of this growth code.

2. *Challenging pride*: Being fair, tolerant, generous or clever.
   . . . These and other values we cherish are, in fact, norms we
   set for ourselves. We try hard of *our own free will* to live up
   to them. And we feel the sting when we do not or cannot.
   Worse still is when *others* give us the feeling of being unfair,
   intolerant, stingy or stupid. Upholding the consumer's pride
   can be a mission for your brand and the way to achieve outstanding growth.

3. *Exposing inconsistencies*: We want all our actions to be
   consistent with our norms and values. When someone exposes
   an inconsistency in our behavior, this becomes a strong
   motivation to correct it. Are consumers spending more
   money and/or time on things that logically should be less
   relevant to them than your product? *Are they setting the
   wrong priorities?* We will show how exposing and straighten-
   ing out an inconsistency can make your brand the logical
   choice.

4. *Overturning taboos*: Some products are taboo because they go
   against our norm of shame, i.e. it is embarrassing to be seen
   with them, like a hemorrhoid ointment or denture cleaner.
   The brand that defeats a taboo once and for all keeps a unique
   edge.

## 1. Eliminating Guilt

We all have a little "book of rules" in our minds that tells
us exactly what is the right thing to do in dealing with other
people – with our companion, the kids, the parents, neighbors,
family and friends. The same applies to our relations also
*vis-à-vis* superiors, officials, people in need and even complete
strangers. The "book of rules" is unforgiving: forget to do the
right thing and the result is a burning sense of guilt. And it

will keep stinging, too, until you do something about it. The same "book of rules" also tells us, for instance, how to conduct ourselves at a cocktail party: what to wear, what to bring as a gift, what to talk about, what subjects to avoid, when it is appropriate to leave. Greeting and farewell rituals, in particular, are very much set in stone. Do the wrong thing and feel the sting of guilt!

There are even more nuances when it comes to the do's and don'ts of interactions within the family. Am I spending enough time with the kids? Are they getting enough pocket money? Do we have to visit Mom and Pop for Christmas? We have pretty clear ideas on what the answers to these questions are (or should be!). Our motivation to do the right thing comes from a sense of social obligation or propriety, a sense of responsibility and an inner conviction. That is why guilt stings us when we forget our parents' wedding anniversary, miss Mother's Day, or cannot fulfill a child's most ardent wish. It is the same guilt we feel when we call home from the office to say we will be late – again.

Brands that reduce or eliminate guilt offer a compelling purchase motive. Winning brands realized that long ago. Let us look at the growth code.

---

### The Guilt Principle

*Position your brand as the means to eliminate the guilt that occurs in your consumer's relationships with others (family, friends, peers, etc.).*

Success factors:

1. *Intensity*: Your brand can only be an antidote to a feeling of guilt that actually exists. Find out how deep it is. Towards whom does the consumer feel guilt? Is it someone your consumer feels close to – a com-

panion, children, friends, neighbors and even pets. The more significant that "other," the better.

2. *Credibility*: Your brand must be perceived as the most credible alternative for eliminating the guilt. What is the evidence to prove your brand can do the job? Your brand is in fact making up for something consumers have not done or cannot do – they cannot risk further disappointment on the part of those they feel guilty about. The willingness to pay a *premium price*, for instance, suggests a stronger appreciation of the other we feel guilty about neglecting.

The effectiveness of the guilt principle is often underestimated. It is also a tool that must be wielded with caution because it works with a powerful human emotion – keep a sense of proportion in terms of dramatizing the guilt and its elimination! How this can be achieved is illustrated by the success of a packed lunch product for the US market.

## Case in point: Lunchables (USA)

When Lunchables was first introduced, the convenience of a ready-packed, healthy lunch for kids made it an instant success with moms and kids alike. However, increasing competition from newcomers who undercut Lunchables' price threatened the brand's number one position in the market. The bonus of being the "original" no longer had any pull in the market; it was now one convenience product among many. After 18 months of steadily declining sales, Lunchables was running out of options.

The brand took a hard look at the product benefit: convenience was actually what made Lunchables interchangeable and precluded any attachment to the brand. The main product benefit had run out of steam.

What Lunchables then zeroed in on was the fact that moms were *feeling guilty* because they did not have the time to prepare a nice lunch for their kids. It was always the same egg salad sandwich hastily prepared between a phone call and the waiting school bus. Lunchables seized the opportunity to position wholesomeness and variety not as simple product benefits, but as a means of eliminating guilt. The new strategy increased sales by 40% within the first year.

We have just seen how the guilt principle can unleash potent market forces. It is also a strategy that is not limited to very few, specific or otherwise special brands – as one might suspect – but can be applied to a broad spectrum of products and services. Like greeting cards, for instance. . . .

## Case in point: Hallmark (USA)

Hallmark's sales were declining and the brand just could not seem to do anything about it. Consumers were obviously not willing to pay the premium for Hallmark design, paper and print quality.

The brand was confronted with the fundamental truth that applies to greeting cards: it is the thought that counts. Consumers were saying, "Why pay extra for a Hallmark greeting card, when it's all about the greeting and not the card." The problem seemed insurmountable and everything pointed to a strategy the brand simply could not afford: a lower price. Would you believe that the Guilt Principle could be a way out? Imagine that it is your mother's birthday and you want to buy her a greeting card. You see the beautiful Hallmark cards, but look at the ones that are a dollar cheaper. And this is what triggers the guilt feeling: how can you possibly want to save money on someone very dear to you? And what if that someone got the feeling he or she was not even worth a Hallmark? Here is a feeling of guilt that can be eliminated – "Hallmark. If you care enough to send the very best." Now, imagine the recipient flips the card and sees that it is not a Hallmark – would that not also imply that the sender did not also care enough? Here, the brand accentuates the feeling of guilt that comes from buying anything but the most expensive greeting card. In fact, the premium pricing *actually* reinforces the strategy – what had been a purchase barrier now becomes an even more compelling purchase motive.

Guilt is not a feeling you can stimulate; the key is to identify where and when this feeling arises and how your brand can contribute towards *eliminating* it.

## 2. Challenging Pride

We now turn to norms and values that we apply to ourselves. "I should be tolerant – and not so conservative." "I should be generous – and not so stingy." "I should be 'with it' – and not so old-fashioned." These are just a few examples of the many norms all of us can relate to. Some are important to us, others less so. Once we have accepted norms for ourselves, we try to live up to them. Abiding by these voluntary codes of conduct is a matter of pride. We congratulate ourselves when we do so successfully, and feel the sting when we do not. The more important a norm is to an individual, the stronger the pride in living up to it.

Our pride gets hurt when we cannot meet our own self-imposed expectations. In other words, when we have overestimated ourselves. Or even worse, when others find out and point out to us that we are not as tolerant as we believe, or as generous, or as hip. . . . This stings our sense of pride and we hasten to prove that they are wrong – i.e. that we are *not* intolerant, *not* stingy, *not* old-fashioned at all!

In the lobby of a Stockholm movie theater there is a sign on the wall that reads, "Old and feeble ladies are permitted to keep their hats on during the movie presentation." This seemingly friendly concession actually touches a vulnerable spot in many female senior citizens. Of course, they would actually rather keep their hats on inside, but keeping them on would automatically point them out as old and decrepit. This stings their pride, creating a strong motivation to take their hat off anyway. The sign actually achieves the intended behavioral change – and no doubt much more effectively than any friendly request or even a blunt ban.

What we pride ourselves in being or not being is a strong motivator. It is a button the people who know us well sometimes do not hesitate to push – and it happens often enough in our every-day interactions. Typical situation: she wants to go camping in the wilderness to celebrate their wedding anniversary; he wants a quiet few days at a luxury resort. Her strategy is to provoke his pride: "Come on, darling, don't be so stuffy, we can do that 30 years from now. Besides, staying at a resort is probably what Sanders and his wife would do." Even if it is a small sting, he feels it and wants to make it go away. The last thing he wants anybody to think, least of all his wife, is that he is no longer up to roughing it a little in the wilderness. Just one example among thousands of how challenging pride can lead us to take a different action.

This also highlights another important aspect of the mechanics of pride: *the reference group*. It is not by coincidence that his wife drops Sanders' name. She knows that being compared with Sanders is an irritating thought for her husband and will tilt the scale in favor of a weekend in the wilderness. *The reference group determines to which degree our pride is challenged.* Falling short of a reference group we feel at least equal or even superior to makes us vulnerable. The further we are behind, the more urgent our need to prove the contrary – and to prove it through action.

---

## The Pride Principle

*Challenge your consumers' pride and position your brand as the means of satisfying it.*
Success factors:

1. *Link*: Connect a particularity of your product or service to your consumer's pride – this can be a strength, a neutral aspect or even a negative.

2. *Soft spot*: Your consumer's pride must be vulnerable where you challenge it. But keep in mind that putting the *consumer* on the spot is not the point: ultimately, your brand is what satisfies your consumer's pride.

3. *Reference (group)*: Establish the right frame of reference: Will being compared with that group elicit a sense of inadequacy on the part of your consumers? Note, that pride stings most when you fall behind a group that you feel superior to. Your consumers should feel at least equal or superior to that reference group.

4. *Authority*: The consumer must *accept* where the challenge is coming from. This is not necessarily your brand or your company. A respected personality in the public eye or even your consumer's peers can sometimes be even more effective in challenging consumers on your behalf.

---

If you are not yet convinced that pride can be a powerful lever, read on to find out how a phone company turned a nation of savers into a nation of investors . . .

## Case in point: Deutsche Telekom (Germany)

As Deutsche Telekom was preparing to go public on the German stock market, the company was looking for private investors to buy shares totaling DM 15 billion. At that time only 5% of the German population owned stocks (compared with 21% in the United States and 17% in the United Kingdom, for instance). The psychological barriers of stock ownership were so strong that rational arguments on better financial returns simply were not enough to convince Germans. They were staunch savers, not investors. Deutsche Telekom was facing a tough challenge: not only did they have a new product to sell, they basically also had to create a market – and create it in the face of much consumer reticence.

What was the big idea? *Deutsche Telekom challenged the pride of "keeping up with the Jones's."* Who are the Jones's here: it's not just the neighbors – it's the whole population! How did Telekom drive home the message? They staged their initial public offering (IPO) as a crusade of the whole nation to the stock market. Anybody who doesn't get on board, will invariably feel left out. And that's what stings their pride.

Imagine everybody around you sees no problem in buying stocks – from the local fire brigade to taxi drivers to the waitresses in a deli – what does that make you? This is, how the inner sting of pride motivated hundreds of thousands to join Deutsche Telekom in going to the stock market.

The strategy's success exceeded all projections: more than 3.1 million people signed for stocks – most of whom had never owned a stock certificate before – more than four times what the banking professionals had estimated to be the maximum number of prospects. In total, the campaign created a demand for DM 100 billion, resulting in an oversubscription factor of six. Deutsche Telekom succeeded in creating more new stock owners than any other public company in Germany.

The case study shows that pride strategies can impact purchase decisions more powerfully than the promise of a benefit. Here, a sound investment (benefit) is superseded by pride ("I don't want to fall behind"). The effectiveness of these strategies hinges on finding the right nerve, the most sensitive spot. How pressing the right button can solve even the most difficult challenge is shown by the following case study.

## Case in point: City of Berlin – Anti-vandalism Initiative (Berlin, Germany)

Graffiti on walls, busses and subways is a big city plague. In Berlin, hefty fines, more surveillance cameras, more guards and attack dogs – nothing seemed to make a difference. And pressure from citizens was rising.

Marching in with big artillery, so to speak, seemed only to compound the problem: vandals are self-proclaimed rebels, underdogs and tough crack-downs only made them martyrs. Not only do they ignore warnings and threats, they laugh out loud at them. So how do you solve the problem? Repression was obviously not working, so what could prevention look like?

The first step was to get a clear picture of what kind of people the city was dealing with. The psychological profile showed that the vandals' actions betrayed cowardice and insecurity; they were thumbing their noses at authority but never in daylight and out in the open. They celebrated themselves as anti-heroes.

*And here is exactly where we can challenge their pride: by exposing them as losers of the sorriest kind!* We want to challenge their pride to such a degree, that ceasing and desisting becomes the only choice.

One of the crucial questions is about the authority that is challenging their pride. For obvious reasons, it can't be the City of Berlin. But what if it were the same people that had so far admired the vandals: their own friends and peers! The ridicule and disdain from their own kind will burst the vandals' pseudo-hero bubble. But how do you make that point? Imagine a cinema commercial that starts like a thriller: a suspenseful, rhythmic cop theme builds up the tension and atmosphere. We see a mangy street dog, scared and hopeless, slinking along the walls and down a subway stairway. We then cut to a vandal armed with spray cans slinking along the same walls and down the same subway steps. Cut to the dog looking around furtively. Cut to our vandal looking around just as furtively. Cut back to the dog lifting a leg and peeing against the wall. And now cut to the vandal spraying graffiti. Already the kids in the audience are hooting – and the silent ones are those who recognize themselves. The hooting and jeering only makes the sting burn hotter. To top it off, the next thing we see in big white letters on a black background: "Every dog has its day."

## 3. Exposing Inconsistencies

Has anybody ever accused you of being *inconsistent?* The accusation always stings. As much as we contradict ourselves, we do in fact aspire to consistency, harmony between thought and action.

Of course, no human being is totally consistent all of the time, it is in our nature and we accept that shortcoming.

What we cannot accept, however, is being *confronted* with an inconsistency. What does an environmental affairs official answer when asked why she drives a car that does not get more than eight miles per gallon? What does the security guard say when you point out to him that he left his front door open and his car unlocked?

If it is sharp enough and hot enough, the sting of an inconsistency will drive us to action – and to the choice of a specific brand. Your brand can also be positioned to resolve an inconsistency. What could that inconsistency be? One place to look is in the consumer's *priorities.* Are consumers spending more money and/or time on things that logically should be less relevant to them than your product? *Are they setting the wrong priorities?* Here is how an insurance company, a foot bath or a charity could approach the issue . . .

- "Your house, your car, your furniture . . . everything's covered, but why aren't you covered against loss of earnings?"

- "You spend so much on shampoos, facial cremes, body lotions . . . and yet you spend nothing on taking care of your feet even though they suffer more abuse."

- "How can you justify donating *more* money to the local outdoor club, of which you're not even a member, than to a charity for starving children in the Third World?"

Inconsistencies like these, when they are exposed for all to see and judge us by, will motivate us to right the wrong. Here is how your brand can be positioned to achieve this consumer goal and win market share in the process.

## The Inconsistency Principle

*Point out an inconsistency in your consumer's priorities and position your brand as the means of resolving it.* Success factors:

1. *Acceptance*: The inconsistency must sting once your consumers are made aware of it. Do they accept it or is it easy to rationalize?

2. *Authority*: The inconsistency must be exposed by a *respected* authority. This is not necessarily your brand or your company. A respected personality in the public eye or even your consumer's peers can sometimes be even more effective in exposing an inconsistency on your behalf.

3. *Credibility*: Your brand must effectively *resolve* the inconsistency. What makes your brand better, more effective than the competition in achieving that goal?

An American life insurer provides a telling example of how to seed this growth code.

## Case in point: Aetna (USA)

Aetna Life & Casualty Co. was confronted with a serious problem. Sales of its life insurance products were down in the face of cheaper competition, but also because of low product relevance in their consumer universe. Research showed that, surprisingly, consumers were spending more time and money on things that should in fact have a lower priority than making sure you are financially secure in your retirement. Aetna's strategy was to draw the consumer's attention to this interesting, if not unsettling, inconsistency: "The average vacation is two weeks, the average retirement is 20 years. How come you take more time to plan a vacation?" A clear case of misplaced priorities: a vacation cannot be *more* relevant than life after work. Millions of consumer feel the sting of this inconsistency and are motivated to resolve it. Aetna positions itself as the logical choice: just call this number and let us get this worry off the table. The strategy resulted in above-average growth.

## 4. Overturning Taboos

Some products stay longer than they probably should on shelf because it is socially suspect to be seen with them. Consumers may find these products necessary and even very useful, but they do not buy them in the appropriate quantity or with the frequency they feel they should. Norms flash on in the mind and say "This is immoral!" or "It's embarrassing!" or simply "This is just wrong!" Erotica (condoms, male potency aids, etc.), female hygiene products (tampons, incontinence products), but also certain medications like hemorrhoid salves or denture products are obvious candidates. But what about retirement homes, burial services or antidepressant drugs? Ultimately, all these products and services find a buyer, of course. What if you could significantly increase the universe of buyers and the frequency with which these products are bought or services are used – and made *your* brand the logical choice in the process? The following growth code points out the key factors in successfully overturning the taboos that loom large in the consumer's mind.

## The Taboo Principle

*Overturn the taboo your brand is associated with by proving how* spectacularly unspectacular *it is.*
Success factors:

1. *Significance*: The taboo you are addressing must be clearly defined – it must also be the main reason for low sales. The bigger the taboo, the greater the potential benefit to your brand.

2. *Anticlimax*: Your brand must make the taboo implode. The bigger the taboo, the bigger the uproar at overturning it. The key is to *defuse* the drama by proving how *spectacularly* unspectacular your brand is! This will make the taboo vanish instead of just toning it down.

3. *Authority*: The taboo must be overturned by an authoritative and credible instance. Since taboos are social norms that are deeply ingrained in a society's conscience, they can only be overturned by a respected authority (an individual or a group) or society as a whole. Ideally, the authority that overturns the taboo is one the consumer least expected.

You will also see that your complete and utter victory over the taboo will reinforce your brand's authority in the consumer's mind – and make your brand the logical choice. The following example shows how the taboo principle works in practice?

## Case in point: Phillips Milk of Magnesia (USA)

Milk of Magnesia was a tried and trusted laxative – except that it was old-fashioned and did not show any significant advantages over other similar products. Sales were slipping. Where could the brand start looking for a solution? That an overnight laxative was dependable was not exactly what people wanted to hear. Since the brand could not build on a quality advantage to make the product more attractive to consumers, Phillips looked at what barrier was *keeping consumers from buying it*. The product was taboo: people were embarrassed to buy it, to talk about it, and to have the need to use it.

Phillips' strategy was to take the taboo head-on: by proving how *spectacularly unspectacular* digestion problems are, they overturned the taboo. Here is how they did it. Imagine a middle-aged couple representing a cross-section of America.

Wherever these two show up, the wife openly talks about her husband's constipation. He is sitting there, so mortified that he would rather die right there and then. In a lovingly awkward way, he gently tries to get his wife off the subject – in vain. Nothing will keep her from sharing her constipation anecdotes.

Here is a typical scene. They are sitting in a restaurant. The waiter comes to the table and that is the perfect excuse for getting started on her favorite subject. The anecdote culminates in a piece of motherly advice to the waiter to have *Milk of Magnesia* put on the menu. At this point, where talking about constipation has our alarm bells ringing the loudest, comes the anticlimax that makes the taboo so spectacularly unspectacular. Sure, why not? Let's put it on the menu.

It so effectively defuses the taboo that we wonder what the fuss was about to begin with. By being the first one to completely and utterly overturn the taboo, Phillips gained a stature in the consumer's mind that competitors would not be able to match.

As we have seen, the taboo principle hinges on making the product spectacularly unspectacular. The authority you put in charge of overturning the taboo is crucial to success. Here are some candidates for the job.

1. Have a *well-known personality* (whom your consumers least expect) admit in all candor to needing or using an "embarrassing" product. Example: famous people speaking openly and freely about life with a hearing aid. The target group can only draw this conclusion: "If these important people in public life are not embarrassed to wear a hearing aid, then why should I be?"

2. Prove that your product naturally belongs in the everyday life of a *highly regarded social group* (e.g. heads of state, CEOs, millionaires, racecar drivers, photo models, doctors). Take a denture cleaner, for example, a typical "taboo" product. One new brand did the unthinkable when it introduced itself: it took us inside a high society household where we see a very distinguished lady deliberately and unselfconsciously dropping a denture cleaning tablet into the glass on her night table, right next to expensive perfumes and cosmetics.

3. Use *statistics* to prove that the taboo you are dealing with does not concern a minority that has to live in hiding. Even if your consumers do not share it with 100 million people, a problem they share with 10 million people is nothing to be embarrassed about.

The evidence is there that even generic or no-name brands became market leaders with the Taboo Principle. There is, of course, no denying the fact that overturning the taboo against using your product will also make competing products acceptable to the consumer. Here, market experience has shown that the brand that is the first to wield the axe – or simply the bigger axe – and chop down the taboo will maintain a unique edge over competitors. *Your* brand is the one that freed consumers of a taboo and they tend not to forget it.

## SUMMARY

Norms and values not only tell us what to do and not to do, but also what to buy and what not to buy. The need to live up to a norm can override even the prospect of a personal benefit. Though most people do not willfully reject a benefit, they will find it impossible to go against what their values and norms dictate. How does your brand fit into this context?

1. Is your brand in a position to eliminate the guilt that your consumer may feel towards others?
2. Is there a way you can challenge – and satisfy – the pride of your consumers?
3. Are inconsistencies in consumer behavior hurting sales – can you point them out?
4. Are any taboos limiting your consumer universe or restricting purchase frequency?

As we have seen, the growth codes behind the Norms & Values portal are just as hard-selling as purely quality or benefit-oriented strategies. They open new opportunities for understanding and identifying an ulterior motive behind choosing one brand over another.

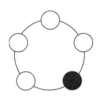

# Portal 3: Perceptions & Programs

**Premise:** *Consumers prefer your brand because behavior and perception programs point to it as a logical choice.*

Where the optimist sees the glass as half full, the pessimist sees it as half empty. It is a matter of perception, and it varies from one person to the next. Modern psychology speaks of *programs* in our minds that guide the way we perceive things and the way we behave. These programs are not installed from outside – our perceptions and actions are *not* remote-controlled. "Program" as it is used here refers to a mind routine for perceiving, collecting and interpreting experiences. A similar type of routine determines our purchase decisions, i.e. whether we are attracted to or indifferent to a brand.

The important issue here is that these perception and behavior programs are not set in stone, but are in a constant state of flux. They can be updated or overwritten. What does this mean in marketing terms? It means that the consumer's perception of your brand can be updated or overwritten with the objective of linking the brand to a compelling purchase motive. Perception leverages sales. Programmed perceptions and actions can neither be explained by Benefits & Promises, nor by Norms & Values. What we are dealing with here are deeply ingrained patterns – like routines, habits and traditions – that your brand can shape together with the consumer. Let us now explore the possibilities behind the Perceptions & Programs portal.

## THE POWER OF HABITS AND ROUTINES

A good portion of our everyday lives reads like a catalogue of actions we would have difficulty *explaining*. For instance:

- *Cultural traditions*: How come breakfast is different from country to country, even region to region? And why do northern Europeans prefer to drink beer in the evening while southern Europeans have a glass of wine? The answers lie in routines that are deeply ingrained in decades and centuries of cultural heritage. These habits are so strong that they are very hard to break.

- *Daily routines*: If we checked all the things we do during the course of day for a clear benefit, we would probably break down with a decision overload. Going to the supermarket and making the optimum choice of cereal would be a nightmare. Here, too, a program in your mind kicks in to whittle the overwhelming variety down into a *relevant set* for purchasing.

- *The force of habit*: Why does an older novelist or journalist still prefer to work with a typewriter rather than a computer? Using a word processing program is much easier, more flexible and much more forgiving. There are many similar examples. People simply have a hard time breaking habits – even if it would make their life a lot easier.

To put it in a nutshell: we do not act as rationally, as purposefully, as we sometimes would like to. And many of these "irrational" behavioral patterns defy explanation. When asked why we do certain things a certain way, the best answer we can give is, "Well, I've been it doing this way ever since I can remember. . . ."

## THE POWER OF PERCEPTION PROGRAMS . . .

Perception is not an objective process but the result of subjective programs. Some of them are present at birth, others are acquired over time. For instance: What is a hammer? "Why, it's a tool for driving nails into a hard surface," you would say. Of course, you would be right, but is that the only *valid* answer? Show the same hammer to someone who lives deep in the Polynesian jungle and has never seen one, however, and he might see in it a *weapon*. A child would first see in it an exciting new *toy*. The fact that most people on this planet see the hammer as a tool is ultimately a shared perception, a routine that is deeply ingrained in our minds. By and in itself the object is "only" a lump of metal attached to a wooden grip – or, even more fundamentally, a juxtaposition of millions of molecules of wood and metal.

The example of the hammer points to another aspect of how we perceive things: the *value* and *desirability* of an object is also determined by a program. Imagine an old clay vessel on sale at a flea market. The first prospect to come along sees a *flower pot* for the kitchen window – he offers the seller US$10. Then along comes an antique collector. This one, recognizing the craftsmanship, sees in the vessel the remnant of a past civilization, a *work of art* from a forgotten culture. He wants this object for much more intense reasons than the first customer and already pictures the precious object standing in a glass cabinet in the middle of his living room. He offers the merchant US$1000. The difference between US$10 and US$1000 is simply perception.

## . . . AND HOW THEY CAN CHANGE

Mental programs can be radically rewritten, too. Here is an authentic story. It is 1847 and we are in the office of Governor Gomm, the Governor of the Island of Mauritius. To commemorate the fifth anniversary of his government, he commissions the post office to produce a special commemorative stamp in a limited edition of 500 blue ones and 500 red ones. The engraver, however, is so overworked that he makes a historical mistake: instead of "Post Paid," it says "Post Office." Ironically, this little mistake has made the "Mauritius" the most precious postage stamp on this planet today. At the last auction, two pristine Mauritius stamps went to a collector for about US$3.5 million. How can it be? It still says "Two Pence" on each. The stamp has not changed, apart from the fact that the paper has aged. What has changed is our perception of it. We no longer see it as a two-pence stamp for sending away a letter, but instead a precious object that must be kept safely in a vault. The astronomical increase in value ultimately results from a tacit agreement among experts, which is respected by millions of individuals on this planet. Today, we are programmed to view this little square of paper as a precious rarity. And if anybody ever had the idea of sticking a Mauritius on an envelope and sending it away, he or she would no doubt be considered insane.

## CHANGING PERCEPTION PROGRAMS IS SOMETHING WE ALL DO EVERY DAY

Most perception and behavior programs are written between the minute we are born and adulthood – through our cultural background, education, upbringing and socialization. And yet, most programs are not rigid, but quite flexible. In everyday life, when we want others to do things – or not do them – we find ourselves trying to change their point of view. What we are in fact doing is trying to reprogram their perception of a situation. In *The Adventures of Tom Sawyer*, Mark Twain shows us how easy this is and how amazing the results can be. . . . Tom has again infuriated his Aunt Polly with some prank and this time his punishment is to paint the long picket fence around the house. Having to paint the fence is bad enough, but suffering the ridicule of his pals is even worse. Sure enough, one of his friends stops by on his way to go fishing and soon makes fun of Tom. It must have been something really serious this time if Tom has to paint the whole fence to make up for it. Tom, clever boy that he is, sees an opportunity to get out of doing the chore. He changes his friend's perception of the situation: *painting the fence is not punishment; it is a rare privilege.* Suddenly, mockery turns into envy. And sure enough, more and more children not only see painting the fence from a completely new perspective, but they even beg Tom to paint the fence for him! Before long all the kids in the neighborhood are trading their most precious belongings for a few brush strokes. By suppertime, the fence has three coats of paint and our Tom is the "wealthiest" little boy in town.

Programmed perception can have far-reaching consequences, as demonstrated by a survey of surgeons that yielded the following interesting statistics. When asked, "Would you operate if the patient had a 10% chance of dying?" most surgeons flatly said no. Rephrasing the question to, "Would you operate if the patient has a 90% chance of survival?" was met with resounding approval. Programmed perception apparently can even decide on the fate of an individual in the operating room.

Here is another anecdote, this one from the history books. Following the Battle of Waterloo, General Blücher, the commander in chief of the Prussian Army, also wanted to blow up the Pont de Jéna (Jéna Bridge) – named after a humiliating Prussian defeat against the French army. Talleyrand, France's foreign minister, had a stroke of genius and renamed the bridge, "Pont de l'École Militaire" ("Bridge of the Military Academy"). He reprogrammed Blücher's perception by "changing" a bridge that symbolized something negative into a bridge that symbolized something positive. The bridge was not blown to bits.

Just two examples of how easily negative perception programs can be changed into positive ones. The key is that the new perception must be accepted by all.

## HOW PERCEPTION IMPACTS THE BOTTOM LINE

Whether a brand sells or stays on the shelf often simply depends on a program in the consumer's mind. It can also make the difference between double-digit or triple-digit sales growth. Just how a better understanding of programs can be leveraged into more sales is shown in the example of a simple cough drop. The consumer's perception, "This is cough medication," determines that this particular cough drop is only purchased and used when cough symptoms appear, i.e. maybe up to three times a year. But what if we altered the consumer's perception and made a case for the product as a refreshing new kind of candy? All of a sudden, the cough drop becomes something you can enjoy all year long, whenever you feel like candy. What happened here? We moved the product out of the mental drawer labeled, "Cough Medication" and into the one labeled, "Candy." Reprogramming a perception can and will increase sales dramatically – as long as the proposition makes sense to the consumer.

Countless products and services fail in the marketplace because the consumer sorts them into the "wrong" mental drawer or into no drawer at all. For each and every need we open a mental drawer and sift through products and services – to find the one that will satisfy that particular need. When I feel a cold coming on, I open the "Cold Medication" mental drawer and what I find is a decongestant brand, a cough syrup brand, an inhalation brand, a cough drop brand, etc. All these brands have a high probability of being bought. Conversely, other products that are just as therapeutic (like a cold relief bubble bath, for instance) but are not stored in this mental drawer will have the highest probability of *not* being considered. Items and brands that are not stored in a mental drawer simply do not exist in the consumer's mind. Versatile, complicated and abstract products – or services – in particular have a tough time winning the consumer's choice because they do not fit into a drawer, or, worse, because they try to fit into more than one drawer.

## THE GROWTH CODES FOR PERCEPTIONS & PROGRAMS

Some of the world's greatest brands owe their success to reprogramming the consumers perception. Here are your options:

1. *Marking your territory*: Mark a (smaller) territory within your overall market in which your brand will be the top dog and still achieve higher sales volume. Let your competitors eat each other up outside your territory.

2. *Cutting into another market*: Does your market offer limited growth potential? Then cut into a new, larger market where your previous weaknesses might even turn into strengths. This approach offers not just one, but two growth codes for altering your consumers' perception of where you belong and opening new horizons for brand growth.

3. *Redefining your league*: Whether you are a major player or not also depends on whether you are playing in the right league. Position your brand in the league in which it is the star player. Here, the new frame of reference actually defines your product or service as having the edge. There are two principles for entering into a completely new ball game – and rewriting the rules.

4. *Inverting a negative*: Are the weaknesses consumers perceive in your brand *really* weaknesses? Are the strengths they perceive in your competitor's product *really* strengths? You can turn a perceived liability of your brand into an asset by changing the consumer's perception. The converse is true when it comes to effectively fending off competitors.

5. *Resetting routines*: Press the reset button on current consumption patterns and "reboot" your brand with a whole new set of usage routines. Here, redefining perceptions will unlock usage restrictions in the consumer's mind and expand your growth potential.

Each of these strategic directions is aimed at making your consumer's programmed perceptions accept your brand as the logical choice without touching the *nature* of your product or service. They will effectively persuade consumers to see your brand from a fresh perspective that did not exist before in their minds.

## 1. Marking Your Territory

You are always better off being a big fish in a small pond than a small fish in a bigger one. The same applies in marketing: the smaller your market, the bigger and more important your brand can be. You will see that "smaller" does not necessarily entail lower volume sales. On the contrary.

The territory you mark for your brand within the larger market for your product or service is the territory in which your brand can unfold and take the supreme position. Excedrin for instance is an over-the-counter pain relief medicine brand that moved out of the huge but fiercely competitive general market for pain relief medication. It marked a "new" territory for itself within that larger market: *headache relief* – without changing the formula. Still very large by any standard, the "smaller" territory enabled Excedrin to become synonymous with headache relief. The result: increased sales and market share. What happened here to the program in the consumer's mind?

- Before, the consumer perceived Excedrin as just one among many pain relief medication brands. There was no clear motive or proposition why the consumer should prefer Excedrin to any other brand.

- Marking a new, specific and credible territory, i.e. *headache relief*, alters the consumer's perception of Excedrin into that of a competent specialist that is more effective in fighting a splitting headache than any other pain reliever. This strategy takes Excedrin out of the general market of pain relievers in which the other brands can continue to go at each other's throats.

Here is another interesting aspect of perception programs that shows just how powerful they are. Let us suppose our product is a mild soap that is positioned specifically for intimate hygiene. This territory is clearly delimited against other mild soaps. But would our mild intimate soap be used to wash the face? Probably not, even though the product cannot possibly contain something detrimental to the complexion. In fact, using this mild soap on your face is possibly even a very good idea because it may contain less aggressive or dehydrating cleansers.

Consumers, however, will resist making that leap. The program that kicks in for intimate hygiene is the powerful force that makes consumers respect the territory we have marked for ourselves: using the product on your face is something you just do not do. Our brand has gained an authoritative position that will not be easily challenged.

To those readers who believe this reeks of market segmentation, here is the difference:

- Segmenting the market means *first* identifying a market niche and *then* designing the product to fit that market. In other words: a *product* strategy.

- Marking your territory means starting from an existing *product* and then defining the *territory* in which it will achieve a new and higher importance in the consumer's perception. In other words: a *brand* strategy.

Do not underestimate the Territory Principle: it opens unexpected and creative new inroads into positioning. Why, for instance, has it taken 100 years to market a moisturizer specifically for "skin after 30"?

By defining this age group as a separate territory within the large market of moisturizers, this creme in effect became the logical choice for more than half of the market. Millions of consumers in the market for a moisturizer who were older than 30 now had a compelling reason to prefer this brand to any other similar creme on the market. Most important, the purchase motive is derived from the basic product benefit: this brand has a higher moisturizer content. From a typical product benefit perspective, this *factual* quality has little effect on consumers: What difference does a little more or a little less make? It's still moisturizer!

Here, from a little relevant product feature ("extra moisturizer") you can derive a relevant market territory ("women over 30") which your brand can own. There are countless other brands out there that could proceed down the same road and arrive at different, yet just as clearly defined territories in which they will reign supreme.

Obviously, marking a territory within a market means *renouncing* on a portion of that bigger market. A moisturizer for "skin after 30" will probably not appeal to consumers *under 30*. That is the price for new growth. Call it an investment. And it is worth it if you do your homework and define a large enough territory.

But let us now look at the practical side: what are the things to look out for when marking a new territory for your brand? What are the success factors for making this a winning strategy?

---

## The Territory Principle

*Look at the general market for your product or service and mark a clearly defined territory in which your brand becomes the logical choice for your consumer.*

Success factors

1. *Relevance*: Your new territory must be relevant. You can derive it from (a) brand particularities (b) unfulfilled consumer needs and/or (c) market gaps.

2. *Demarcation*: What is the *one specific criterion* that sets your new territory apart from the rest of the market? For example, age group, gender, usage.
   . . .

3. *Potential*: Get a precise handle on the size of your new territory, on its consumer universe. Make sure this new territory offers sufficient growth opportunities for the long term.

4. *Credibility*: Make sure your brand is clearly perceived as the authoritative product in your new territory. Look at the facts in your brand and use them as evidence so that others cannot kick you out.

There are different ways of marking your own territory. For example, by focusing on usage:

- Application areas (e.g. a deodorant specifically intended for *feet*)

- Application occasions (e.g. a breakfast snack for *on the go*)

- Application times (e.g. a cough medication for *night-time*)

- Problem intensity (e.g. a relief medicine against *light* headaches)

- Problem phases (e.g. a relief medicine against *early* flu symptoms)

Or by focusing on consumer characteristics:

- Age (e.g. a toothpaste range for *specific life stages*)
- Gender (e.g. a facial creme for *men*)

- Education, income, profession, social status (e.g. a stir and serve meal for *executives*)

- Origin, culture, nationality (e.g. potato chips for *Hispanics*)

- Interests, hobbies, habits (e.g. a vitamin boost for *smokers*)

This list is far from exhaustive. There are no limits to creativity in defining the right territory for your brand. The following case illustrates how this strategy can help you think outside the box and arrive at a completely unexpected territory for your brand.

## Case in point: Felix (UK)

From a quality standpoint there is not much to differentiate Felix from other cat foods. And yet Felix manages continuously to strengthen its position in the market. The brand did not position itself on quality or "taste," but on a programmed perception in the cat owner's mind. The key was to reach beyond quality and think in terms of a territory.

The success story began as Felix market researchers set out into the real world to chat with cat owners. What they discovered: an interesting disconnect between the way cat owners described their feline companions and the way most competitors portrayed cats. Cat owners would talk about their cats as being individual, strong-willed, clever and even a bit mischievous, whereas Felix' competitors saw cats as the tender, cuddly objects of cat owners' attention.

What emerged was a territory within the market that Felix could mark and dominate: *all cats with character.* The necessary sacrifice: cuddly cats that have no character can happily grow fat and content with the competitor's fare. Now what happens in the cat owner's mind? Those with a cat with character will naturally gravitate towards Felix. And those who wish their cat had more character will as well. Felix is now the logical choice for a large consumer universe. The brand defined a large enough territory for itself – one in which Felix could grow and be the uncontested leader, and the success was spectacular. Within 10 years market share increased sixfold from approximately 5% to just under 30%. Felix became the number one brand among cat foods and actually ranked among the fastest growing brands in Britain.

Today, Felix is one of the 30 best-known brands in Britain and looking to expand internationally. This is all the more amazing when you consider that Felix did not have to *prove it was of superior quality*. Felix drove the idea home to consumers with a cartoon cat that is always up to some (charming) mischief – which underscores character. One spot shows us the missus on the phone chatting with her neighbor. Felix charms and purrs his way around her and up onto the sideboard and then just plunks his paw on the receiver – "My turn now!" we can imagine him meowing. "Cats like Felix like Felix." – more than just a compelling tagline, it sums up the whole strategy.

The case study shows the creative potential in marking a territory vs. taking a segmentation approach. What this also tells us is that the mission of marking a territory within your existing, larger market can inspire a new, unconventional growth opportunity. We are now going to look at a more aggressive variant of the Territory Principle: it will enable you to relegate a dangerous new competitor into a smaller market.

### The Territory Principle (to Reposition Competitors)

*Mark the smallest possible territory in which to relegate your most significant competitor. Now claim the remaining majority of the market for your own brand.*

Success factors

1. *Competitor*: The bigger the threat to your franchise, the more effective the repositioning will be.
2. *Potential*: The narrower the territory you define for your competitor, the more room in the market for your brand to unfold.
3. *Link*: The new territory you are defining for your competitor must be derived from a particularity of their product or service – this may be an apparent strength or weakness.
4. *Home Territory*: Repositioning your competitor is only half the battle – your brand must stake a firm claim on the remaining majority of the market.

This counter-strategy in marking a territory is equally effective. As in martial arts, the secret here is to use your competitor's energy – positioning and marketing budget – and reflecting it back to your advantage. In fact, your competitor will be doing the work of putting *you* on top of the market. The following example shows how to apply this reverse strategy and the spectacular results you can achieve.

Let us say your product is a conventional kitchen towel, nothing special but it does the job and does it well. Most home-makers rely on it and you have a solid market share. Then a new brand enters the market, promising to be much more absorbent and so tear-resistant you can even use it to tow a car. How can you possibly compete? You don't! You mark a new, extremely narrow territory in which the other brand can reign supreme, albeit with a limited opportunity for growth. Here, marking a territory means starting from the competitor's product. Even though it's made for all homemakers, we can rightfully relegate

our competitor to the mini-territory of "extremely messy acci-
dents" – which don't happen that often in normal kitchens. Our
own brand can now claim the remaining majority of the market:
all those normal, everyday wipe-up jobs. By repositioning our
competitor, we are also implying that those who need it must be
pretty sloppy people and have especially filthy kitchens. In other
words: "civilized" households don't need that kind of heavy duty
product.

The Territory Principle can thus be applied to putting a competitor back in his place without even an offensive move on your
part. As in jiu-jitsu, the opponent's own strength and momentum
are used to defeat him.

The Territory Principle looks at ways of creating an exclusive
enclave for your brand *within* the larger market for your type of
product. Felix cat food now has its own territory, but it is still
within the cat food market. The same applies to your kitchen
towel. We are now going to look at how a brand can successfully
venture into a *new, different, perhaps even remote* market and tap
into new growth potential.

## 2. Cutting Into Another Market

For obvious reasons, this approach may be necessary if your
brand can no longer grow as well or as quickly in its current
market. Here are a couple of examples of brand opportunities that
can be realized with this strategy:

- Instead of competing against an army of soft drink brands, a
  cola could position itself as an alternative to tea or coffee for
  breakfast.

- Instead of confining itself to the dessert market, a fresh cheese
  brand could position itself as a low-calorie snack alternative
  to cake, chips, etc.

Explore the possibilities of your brand in terms of being a viable player in a completely different market.

---

### The Expansion Principle

*First target a new, additional market. Then position your brand as an unexpected alternative in that market.*

Success factors:

1. *Acceptance*: Make sure your consumers accept your product as an alternative – it must be able to fulfill the basic need as well as, if not better than, its new competitors.

2. *Uniqueness*: Clearly define the strengths of your product vs. its new competitor line-up. For which occasions, situations, etc. is your product the better choice? Or for which consumer group?

3. *Potential*: The bigger your new competitor line-up, the stronger your chances of acquiring market share at his expense.

4. *Compatibility*: This strategy is not about exchanging one market for another – it is about expanding it. Confirm that your current consumers will not reject your expanded brand universe.

---

The Expansion Principle can lead to amazing, even spectacular, brand strategies for the most unexpected products. Consider what it accomplished for a chewing gum brand. . . .

### Case in point: Wrigley's (USA)

As the absolute market leader, Wrigley's was hitting the limits of growth in the chewing gum market. At the same time, however, new brands appeared, eroding Wrigley's number one position. The strategic leap was to expand into the cigarette market and position Wrigley's as a viable alternative in all those situations where smoking is frowned upon, i.e. at the office, in public places, at the hospital . . . This came at the right time since new regulations were beginning to officially prohibit smoking in certain places. A very original idea, because chewing gum fulfills a similar need. Smoking releases nervous energy in a ritual that goes from reaching into your pocket to taking the cigarette out of the pack to lighting up and taking a long drag. A similar pattern applies to chewing gum, from taking the wrapper off to the chewing experience. Of course, smokers had long been consumers of chewing gum: but Wrigley's discovered the seed, that had been planted, and cultivated it.

The Expansion Principle is one way of cutting into another market. There is also a second way, one that takes a much more radical approach. Here, your brand leaves its traditional home to find a new one in a completely different product category: we call it *migration*. Remember the mental drawers? Migration is about taking your brand out of its current mental drawer and placing it into another. Let us think about the fruit juice we mentioned in the introduction. The consumer finds it too watery, too sweet, too artificial and probably not as healthful *because* it is in the same drawer as Tropicana and other 100% pure fruit juices. Our pseudo-juice has serious drawbacks. Migration means taking our brand out of the juice drawer and putting it in the soft drinks drawer instead. Not only is our brand now a new, refreshing alternative to soft drinks, but it also compares very favorably with them: it is not as sweet, has more real fruit and it is more natural. All of a sudden our doomed brand gets a new, solid lease on life in a completely different environment!

---

### The Migration Principle

*Migrate into a different or even unexpected "mental drawer" where your brand can better unfold.*

Success factors:

1. *Acceptance*: Consumers must accept your brand in the new mental drawer. Bear in mind that they will have new, different expectations of your product.
2. *Potential*: The new category must offer greater growth opportunities than the current one.
3. *Uniqueness*: Make sure you accentuate those characteristics that differentiate your product from your new competition.

---

Italian confectioner Ferrero has been using this principle to migrate from the *sweets* category to the *healthy food* category. For good reasons: first, it was a way out of the cut-throat competition in the confectionery market; secondly, it liberated the brand of the stigma of sweets, i.e. high-calorie, bad for your teeth and your health.

### Case in point: Ferrero Milchschnitte ("Milk Sandwich" Germany)

If we consider only taste and ingredients, there would be no question that *Milchschnitte* belongs in the sweets category that ranges from candy bars to ice cream to gum drops: it is a sweet cream filling with a blend of milk and honey between two biscuits. Ferrero's brand strategy, however, was to position it in the healthy dairy foods category. This is how Ferrero did it:

- The product itself looks very much like a typical sandwich. Two slices of whole-wheat bread and white cream in-between. The designation *Milchschnitte* (Milk Sandwich) reinforces this visual impression.

- The packaging shows a label that says "Main Ingredient: Fresh Milk." Right next to it we see a traditional milk jar and a pot of honey.

- The product is only sold on refrigerated shelves, right next to dairy products (i.e. yogurts, cheese, butter and milk.)

- The product is even endorsed by an independent institute for sports nutrition that recommends *Milchschnitte* as a wholesome snack for athletes.

- The campaign works with real athletes for its testimonials these are not actors who go on record saying that *Milchschnitte* is the lightest, non-filling and most convenient healthy snack.

This strategy has made Ferrero's product one of the top 100 brands in Germany and one that is still growing at double-digit rates.

To summarize: when we enter a new market, we can either expand our franchise against a new competitor (Expansion Principle), or migrate to a completely new category (Migration Principle).

## 3. Redefining Your League

People place products and services not just into mental drawers, but also into specific leagues. Wines, cars, hotels or sports

teams are just a few examples of league thinking from the
consumer's perspective: expensive wines and cheap wines, high-
performance cars and utility vehicles, budget motels and five-
star hotels.

This approach opens yet another avenue for positioning a
product or service for optimum growth. From the consumer's
perspective, the league helps to compare what is on offer and
filter out the relevant set. If your brand is not on the roster, you
do not stand a chance. Some people only book five-star hotels,
only fly business class and only choose wines in the US$20+
range. Anything else is automatically suppressed. Others still,
look for their products and services in the budget league. They
do not even want to know what the next category up has to offer.
In this sense, brand growth also depends on whether the brand
is positioned in the right "league." Here are a few things to
consider:

- Many brands try for a leap from the medium league into
  the premium league. The idea here is to elude the competitive pressures in the mass market and gain share in
  the premium market. Caution: the premium segment
  may be a lot smaller than your market and just as competitive, threatening current sales and limiting further
  growth.

- You can also combine the advantages of two classes: by
  offering premium class quality at medium class prices, for
  instance. Continental Airlines used this strategy to build up
  its Business First product: "To your boss it's Business. To your
  butt it's First."

- Sometimes it can also be useful to create a *new class* that
  does not exist in the consumer's perception. Suppose you
  want to market a new mobile phone. It offers excellent

quality and value, but it is not cutting edge in terms of weight, size and talk time. Market surveys tell you that consumers perceive it at the bottom of the premium class – so consumers will not buy it. Now, what happens if we create a medium class and position it at the top of it?

---

### The League Principle

*Move your brand into a different, unexpected league in which it can fully unfold.*

Success factors:

1. *Acceptance*: Your brand must live up to your consumer's quality, price and value expectations in the new league. Are there specific product features/characteristics to legitimize your presence in that league?

2. *Potential*: Make sure that your new league offers long-term growth opportunities. Beware of maneuvering yourself from a larger market into a smaller universe with limited growth prospects.

3. *Uniqueness*: What is the competition in your new league? Clearly define how your product or service compares favorably against it.

---

The amazing possibilities for applying the league principle are exemplified by Persil, the leading laundry detergent in Germany.

## Case in point: Persil Megaperls (Germany)

The market for laundry detergents is one of the most competitive in Germany, dominated by Persil, with Ariel (Procter & Gamble) a close second. The fight for market share seemed like an endless tug-of-war. Then Persil introduced a surprising innovation: the powder was compressed into little pellets. It was a purely cosmetic change with absolutely no effect whatsoever on detergent capability – the formula had not been altered. And yet this questionable innovation triggered a staggering market success. How could this be? Persil did not just announce "New and Improved!" It called the pellets "Megaperls" and heralded a whole new generation in laundry detergents. The result: competitors were automatically marked down as "the old generation." Persil had established a new league and the Megaperls were the credentials. The net effect is that consumers are not deciding for or against the little pellets, but, instead, for or against a new *generation* of detergent. The strategy helped Persil increase its market lead of 5% versus Ariel (Procter & Gamble) to 8.6%. No small feat in that market.

So much for the League Principle, which in most cases appeals directly to the consumer's logic centers. There is, however, a second way of positioning your product in a different league to address a powerful purchase motive. We call it *magnification*. The idea here is to make your brand part of something bigger, a player in a larger and more significant context – and make your competitors suddenly look insignificant by comparison. Check your brand's potential for magnitude:

- Does it solve a problem of *national* or even *global* significance?

- Is it known even in the most remote corners of the world?
- Does it fulfill an important social mission?
- Does it belong to a nation's cultural heritage? Or
- Has it earned a place in the history books?

You are probably already thinking of a few, carefully selected luxury brands – yes, these would be obvious candidates. However, very mundane, everyday items – from facial tissues to instant coffee to beer – have also become winning brands on the strength of a carefully crafted magnification strategy. Here is how:

---

### The Magnification Principle

*Position your brand within a larger context that magnifies its significance or role. This makes your competitors look small, plain and negligible.*

Success factors:

1. *Relevance:* Your brand's new magnitude must be relevant in the category and to your consumers. (Keep in mind that the youth market often sees "big" as being "uncool" and responds better to underdog brands to further differentiate itself from the mainstream.)

2. *Credibility:* Your brand's new magnitude must have a factual basis.

3. *Precision:* Be as clear as you possibly can about the "important role" your brand plays or has played in society, history, etc. Unclear, ill-defined or abstract magnification quickly loses steam.

4. *Uniqueness*: Magnification works best when your competitors focus their marketing on factual arguments and seem small or provincial. Here, contrast enhances magnification.

In real marketing life there are a number of magnification types that function on their own, but can also be combined:

1. *Cultural or historical magnitude*: Here, we look at brands that have become icons of a specific culture, i.e. products that embody the spirit of a generation or even earn their place in the history books. It does not hurt to relativize this kind of ambitious positioning with a pinch of humor, as the following example shows. German car manufacturer Audi was the first to introduce a volume production car with an aluminum body, a top-of-the-line model called the A8. The strategy was to magnify the innovation in a historical context: after the Stone Age, the Bronze Age and the Iron Age, we have now arrived at the Aluminum Age. It is thus not a launch of a new model, like any other after each model year. It is the dawn of a New Age. Audi increased sales by 24%, while competing models from Mercedes-Benz and BMW lost 13% and 10%, respectively. Magnification also works in completely different industries. American oil company ExxonMobil, then Mobil Oil, used this strategy to reinforce its premium positioning. Mobil was there when Lindbergh crossed the Atlantic. Mobil fuels are used in the Space Shuttle program. Bringing the brand into the context of important historical achievements gives Mobil a legitimate claim to premiumness.

2. *Magnitude by analogy*: Your brand can also gain a new, grander magnitude by analogy. The British Automobile Association (AA) placed itself on the same level as the fire department, the police and the ambulance emergency service by

saying, "To our members, we are the fourth emergency service." The easily grasped analogy places the AA in a higher league – in fact, the highest league of public services. The result is that the confidence, respect and trust enjoyed by these public services now also applies to the AA. It is much more than any other roadside assistance club. The strategy delivered handsome dividends: within a year of airing the campaign, the number of new members trebled from 34 000 to 102 000.

3. *Magnitude by omnipresence*: Does your brand solve problems of a national or global magnitude? Find out to which extent your product is present and/or appreciated in the remotest parts of the world. By delivering "Solutions for a small planet," IBM takes on the call to transform our world into a village. The brand achieves a new, greater magnitude by taking on a societal role. In the brand communication, IBM shows us a lonely Bedouin on a camel who flips open his laptop to get directions around the next pyramid; a monk in a remote Buddhist monastery sending an e-mail to the Pope; or a wildlife preserve guard registering elephant populations on his laptop for a research project. They are all in the middle of nowhere, in an absolutely low-tech environment, with the highest of advanced technology to connect them with the rest of the world. They use high-tech equipment as if it were the most natural thing – thanks to IBM.

To summarize, when we redefine our league, we can either position ourselves in a new class (League Principle), or we can magnify our brand's role in an even larger context (Magnification Principle).

## 4. Inverting a Negative

Clearly the *class* in which a product belongs is not determined by its physical nature, but in the perception in the consumer's mind.

We are now going to think this through and argue that reprogramming perceptions is also an effective means to transform a perceived weakness into a strength. This is about the art of transforming purchase *barriers* into purchase *bridges*. Here we will see that even the most "hopeless" products can successfully stop and reverse a negative sales trend.

---

### The Reinterpretation Principle

*Reinterpret a perceived negative, or a neutral aspect of your brand, into a positive meaning, significance or value that is relevant to the consumer.*

Success factors:

1. *Acceptance*: The consumer is the ultimate instance for the validity of your reinterpretation. Test your strategy.

2. *Relevance*: The resulting positive meaning, significance or value must form a compelling purchase motive. Measure the relevance of this new proposition against what your competitors have to offer.

---

Reinterpreting a product feature into a compelling purchase motive is not restricted to a particular type of product or industry. Slurpee, a frozen soft drink sold by 7-Eleven in the United States is a good example. Typical consumer feedback: "It is so cold it feels like the top of your head just got blown off." Slurpee reinterpreted this negative into a positive value: "So good it hurts." They did it one better and dubbed their product "Brainfreeze." Slurpee became a cult product with young consumers and the expression even entered into the vernacular. This is the idea behind reinterpretation, but the principle can a do a lot more for your brand. You can unleash huge demand for seemingly unsellable products with this strategy, as the following example shows. . . .

## Case in point: Braun (Germany)

When Braun AG, now owned by Gillette, decided to exit the hi-fi market and focus on its core business of electric shavers and household appliances, the company was faced with a problem. There were still thousands of stereo systems in warehouses so that the cost of leaving the market was especially high. Also, objectively speaking, Braun hi-fi systems offered exceptional design, but basically obsolete technology and high prices – sales had never been spectacular to begin with. Braun was looking at a disaster: dealers would slash prices, ultimately hurting the premium image Braun of other products it continued to manufacture. What could Braun do to avoid fire-sale pricing and protect the brand's premium image? The strategic leap was to reinterpret the product from "dead inventory" to "Limited Edition." And so the Braun Last Edition series was born. Each stereo system was ennobled with a special numbered plaque. What until then had been perceived as simple consumer electronics suddenly became a collector's item.

The strategy delivered results beyond expectations. Even Braun's high pricing could be sustained until the last unit was sold. And divestiture costs were reduced by more than 30%. This send-off even leveraged Braun's remaining business, contributing to an overall growth of 16% in sales for the same year.

We have glimpsed how an undeniable weakness in a product can be turned into a selling point. But what if we could transform the strengths of a competitor into weaknesses? . . .

---

### The Reinterpretation Principle (to Reposition Competitors)

*Reinterpret a strength of your key competitor into a negative meaning, significance or value. Contrast your own brand as a positive to that negative.*

Success factors:

1. *Competitor*: Set your sights on the market leader or on a specific group of competing products that the consumer perceives as direct alternatives to your brand. The bigger the "foe" you manage to reposition, the greater the potential for market share gains.

2. *Acceptance*: Your consumer must accept your repositioning of the competitor – it may not be dismissed as an allegation. Deliver the arguments to substantiate it, or your efforts may backfire.

3. *Relevance*: The resulting negative meaning, significance or value must form a compelling purchase barrier. Measure the relevance of this new proposition against what you have to offer.

4. *Contrast*: Do not rely only on your competitor's new negative. Oppose a strength in your product to the weakness you have exposed in your competitor – create a positive contrast.

---

The effect never ceases to be amazing: the competitor's strategy turns into a boomerang. Indeed, there are always two sides to a coin: even the most successful, formidable competitor has an Achilles heel. In fact, the greatest strength may well hide a weakness. Find it and expose it.

## Case in point: Micrografx (USA)

As an edutainment software developer, Micrografx is a modern "David" vs. market giants Sega and Nintendo. The small company is watching sales slip as the two behemoths dazzle kids with mind-boggling shoot'em-up graphics and sounds.

Micrografx seized on a telling market insight: the parents' worst nightmare is to see their children go brain dead playing video games. The opportunity lay in taking the competitors' biggest strength – great entertainment for kids – and reinterpreting it into a negative: *mind-numbing addiction*. Here, Micrografx positions itself as the positive balance against this huge negative on the side of the competition – as the creative, inspiring alternative, the game that actively involves your child and does not just feed it color and sounds.

All of a sudden the arguments used by Sega and Nintendo to sell their products became even more powerful arguments *not to buy them*. The strategy propelled Micrografx to second place in edutainment software sales.

## 5. Resetting Routines

For almost every product we use in our lives there is a *usage manual* stored in our minds somewhere, which tells us *when, how* and *how often* to use certain products or services. *Apfelwein* or apple wine, for instance, which is a German regional beverage made from fermented apple juice, is enjoyed almost exclusively in the *summer* and *outdoors* – preferably in a so-called *Apfel-*

*weingarten.* There is no plausible reason *not* to enjoy Apfelwein during the winter or at home, but it never crosses people's minds to disregard the "usage manual." A pity for the Apfelwein and a pity for those who make it because sales could increase significantly were it not for this mental block. Many products have the same problem: sales are limited by deeply ingrained usage programs – the usage manual in consumers' minds has a very short list of applications for the product. For some brands, the greatest growth potential lies in removing these usage limitations in the mind.

But where do usage manuals come from in the first place? Think about After Eight, a British mint chocolate. The name itself establishes a usage program that consumers may well find difficult to ignore – indulging in an After Eight *before eight* does not come naturally. Lila Pause, a chocolate bar marketed in Germany, also comes with a built-in usage manual because "Pause" (break, time off) hints at enjoying it when you take a break during the workday. Although there is no sensible reason for not enjoying an After Eight during the day or a Lila Pause during the evening, consumers easily accept the program dictated by the name (!) and find no reason to challenge it.

Altering a program that is deeply ingrained in your consumer's mind is not an easy challenge. But we have also seen that it is not an impossible one. Here is the growth code for resetting the routine your consumer associates with your product and increasing its sales and market-share potential.

## The Usage Principle

*Establish a completely new and credible set of clearly defined uses or applications for your brand. Rewrite the usage manual in your consumer's mind.*

Success factors:

1. *Acceptance*: Your consumer must accept the new circumstances (location, time of day, occasions) for
   using or consuming your brand. Beware of addressing a circumstance for which a competitor might be
   perceived as more appropriate.
2. *Potential*: These new usage situations must happen
   frequently in your consumer's everyday life. They
   must be a clear departure from familiar or learned
   patterns – you are creating a new market, but one
   that does not negate your current market.
3. *Role model*: Most usage routines have been learned
   from *authoritative individuals* – parents, friends,
   peers and individuals we admire and respect.
   Use accepted role models to introduce the *new* usage
   patterns.

How do winning brands make the Usage Principle work for them?
Philadelphia cream cheese is a telling example. The statistics
were dismal: 74% of British consumers enjoyed Philadelphia . . .
but only on crackers, as a cocktail snack, in small quantities and
at most once a week. The strategy called for rewriting the usage
manual and adding *breakfast* to the list of occasions. A major challenge because cream cheese historically is not something you
would find on a British breakfast table. Here, role models drove
home a new set of instructions that consumers readily understood
and accepted. Within one year, acceptance of Philadelphia on the
breakfast table increased from 8% to 36%. The following case is
even more spectacular.

## Case in point: Magnum (Europe)

Before Magnum, a Unilever brand, was introduced, ice cream bars were perceived as being for

- kids
- outside (on the beach, in the park)
- once in a while
- during the day
- in the summertime

This usage program was deeply ingrained in the consumer's mind. The brand experts at Uniliver checked this program and found that there really were not any *compelling reasons*, rational or other, for the restrictive usage patterns attached to ice cream bars. Without challenging the set routines, Unilever wrote a new program with additional uses for Magnum and positioned the brand as *also* being for

- adults
- at home
- anytime
- during the evening
- all year round

Magnum installed a whole new, much larger set of usage opportunities for the consumer to choose from. Magnum is now for *all consumers, anytime* and *anywhere*. Within the first year, market share leapt from 8% to 20%. And Magnum now turned into the uncontested market leader.

Resetting routines can free your brand from limiting con-
straints and power it up for new growth. The key is to ensure your
consumer accepts your proposition and adopts it. Take a look at
the current usage manual in your consumer's mind — you might
stumble across a restriction that does not make sense. It is up to
you to rewrite the manual.

## SUMMARY

The consumer's perception programs are a key factor of sales and
market share growth for modern brands. Whether you keep a
cough drop on your tongue only once a year or every day ultimately depends on whether you perceive it as cold medication or
candy. Here are the options for making consumer perceptions
work for you:

1. Marking your territory
2. Cutting into another market
3. Redefining your league
4. Inverting a negative
5. Resetting routines

These are all strategies that provide you with solid arguments to
challenge current perceptions. They offer consumers a fresh and
compelling perspective from which to judge your brand. Experience shows that working with perceptions and programs can generate double-digit sales and market share increases (cf. Chapter
7, Working with growth codes).

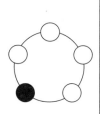

# Portal 4: Identity & Self-expression

**Premise:** *Consumers prefer your brand because it expresses their (desired) character and identity.*

Brands tell us a lot about the character, personality and identity of an individual. This is not only true for car brands, clothes and fashion accessories, but also for cigarettes, body care products and many more. The very first visual impression you get from an individual speaks volumes, and brands very often set the tone.

Here is an experiment: close your eyes and picture a wine-red cardigan, a pair of sandals and a pipe . . . Now describe with as much detail as possible the individual these items could belong to. Already, a surprisingly clear picture is forming in your mind. It is most probably a man, most probably middle-aged, a quiet, mature intellectual type – not a hint of youthful impulsiveness, here. More sedate than hip, he probably also strikes you as more trustworthy, the person you would turn to for advice. He is not into sports, except for the kind on TV and he probably has a potbelly.

Three items is all it takes to get a first impression that is hard to shake. In your mind, you find it hardly a stretch to assume that he is married, has a college-age daughter, lives in a small suburban home and probably teaches at his daughter's college. That also makes him more a liberal than a conservative, someone who enjoys reading and listening to opera. The car in the driveway is slightly battered and he probably calls it a sweet name when he is alone at the wheel. . . . All these suppositions are based solely on the associations triggered by a cardigan, sandals and a pipe.

Right or wrong, typecasting is a natural process. The interesting thing is that superficial objects give us an insight into much deeper aspects of an individual – what his or her values, convictions, even opinions on certain issues might be. A brand is an object with a name and a certain character. By choosing a particular brand, we decide what the objects with which we surround ourselves will tell others about us. What if the cardigan in question were from Armani instead of Pringle? What if the sandals were a high-tech polymer version from Reebok instead of plain leather. And what if the pipe were from Porsche Design instead of Dunhill? It would have triggered a whole new set of associations. *A brand has the potential to comprehensively characterize us in a split-second.*

Imagine a Harley-Davidson driver in terms of

- Gender
- Age
- Character
- Attitude, ideology
- Social status/class
- Way of life, hobbies, habits

As in the other scenario, you could probably tell us exactly what
he or she looks like without ever having seen that person. Of
course, this is all the result of our natural penchant for precon-
ceived notions and typecasting. It is a reflex and there is no way
of turning it off. Consumers are very much aware of what their
purchase decisions tell others about themselves. The brand
becomes an identifier. This identifier function – *which is completely detached from product functionality or quality* – is a powerful purchase motivator to some and a powerful purchase barrier
to others.

Because a brand can be a strong identifier, the consumer will
often disregard a product of better quality and value if owning or
using it sends the "wrong" message. Instead, he or she may well
stick with an average or even below-average alternative if only to
send the "right" message. Brand professionals realize that it is in
the power of the brand to define what this message should be.
This premise is the first step into the fourth portal within the consumer's mind – Identity & Self-expression.

## A FEW THOUGHTS ON IDENTITY . . .

Identity is not only the answer to the question, "Who am I?" but
also to, "Where do I stand in my social context?" In other words,
"What is my position, my situation with regard to my friends,
neighbors, colleagues, the rest of the world . . . ?" It used to be
that family, social class, religion, profession (usually in father's
footsteps) and one's role in a community determined one's identity. Your identity was pretty much mapped out for you – and
staying on that road was pretty much the natural thing to do. Over
the past decades, however, these identifiers have become more
flexible, less clear-cut and certainly no longer as significant.
Where does the expression "to reinvent oneself" come from, if
not from of these changes?

But how do we set about reinventing ourselves? It happens by making certain choices and taking certain actions that become *symbolic* of our identity:

- The first cigarette, the first sexual encounter, moving into one's first own four walls – these choices have a high symbolic value in defining our identity as we step into adulthood.

- The choice of companion is a way of giving one's own identity a new direction. When a commoner marries into a royal household, his or her identity is given a new label that will change it for life.

- Joining a specific group or society – be it a subculture, a club or a church – gives us a new identity. Whether it is the Freemasons, ravers or Hell's Angels, the group of which we become a part is a means of asserting our identity to ourselves and to others.

- To many individuals a mid-life crisis is a time of remodeling an identity that suddenly seems too old, conservative or faded. Here, symbolic actions help them to cope and reinvent themselves – like buying a motorcycle to feel younger, booking a survival trip and walking over hot coals, or finding a new, younger companion.

Some people will do the strangest things to (re)model their identity. What drives American geology student Rip Howell to spend $17\frac{1}{2}$ hours in a bathtub filled with ketchup? Because it will identify him as a World Champion (even if it is in the most inane discipline) and set him apart from the rest of humanity. From average citizen to a paragraph in *The Guinness Book of World Records* in just over 17 hours. Neither a scientific interest in studying the effects of prolonged exposure of the skin to tomato sauce nor even a weird love of ketchup had anything to do with getting into that tub and holding out for that long.

What we consume, because it is visible to others – in the way we dress, in what we put on the belt at the supermarket cashier, in what we put on the table when we have guests, and in what car we sit at the traffic lights – is just as eloquent about our identity as are our actions. This desire to alter, qualify, even amplify one's identity is also one of the motivations behind brand preference. Brands are more than ever an important means of identification. Whether it is adventurous or sophisticated, traditional or trendy, youthful or mature, a brand helps you feel the way you want to feel by identifying you as that type of person.

## THE SOCIAL IMPORTANCE OF SELF-EXPRESSION

Defining your identity is an *inward* process. We now turn to the *outward* process: self-expression. The faster the pace of modern life, the more precious time becomes. That is why we rely more and more on appearances, e.g. brands, to sum others up in our judgment. It is about social positioning. Besides establishing you as affluent, buying a Jaguar car positions you differently from buying a Range Rover or even a New Beetle. If you are single, this will also have an effect on the type of person who might gravitate towards you. More important, brands determine access to, and acceptance by, certain groups – from street gangs to high society clubs. Brands, in other words, give others an advance notice of who you are. In a sense, they do much of the talking for you.

Here is an authentic story. It tells of aging cobbler Wilhelm Voigt who one day acquires a second-hand uniform of a captain in the Prussian army. From there on, he pretty much goes with the flow as the uniform bestows onto him not only the rank of an authentic captain, but also the authority that goes with it . . . Walking down the road, he happens upon a platoon of soldiers led by a lieutenant. Before Voigt can rectify the misperception, the junior officer places himself and his men under the "captain's" command. Our ex-shoemaker quickly lives up to his new rank and has them marching to the village of Köpenick, just eight miles outside Berlin. He is on a roll now – managing even to convince the local police that the mayor and the city treasurer embezzled army funds. Not only does he then appropriate the small fortune of 4000 Reichsmarks, but he also succeeds in having the two town officials arrested and sending "his" troops off to Berlin with the two prisoners.

All this just because of a second-hand captain's uniform.

How and why Voigt took advantage of the situation does not detract from the fact that a simple item of clothing radically repositioned Voigt from cobbler to respected military authority.

Focusing solely on positioning a brand for the consumer ignores a crucial aspect: the brand's role in positioning the consumer.

## TURN YOUR BRAND INTO A MEGAPHONE FOR THE CONSUMER

Many brand images are still being built as *idealized* mirrors for their consumers: they reflect *composites* of attributes, such as youthful, active, individualistic, bold, etc. – the so-called psychographic profile. People who identify with a particular composite image, so the theory goes, will prefer the brand that projects it. Decades ago, Coca-Cola was one of the first brands to benefit from this so-called mirror approach by projecting to the young market a reflection of itself: "You are youthful, active, athletic, fun- and leisure-oriented – you are the Coca-Cola Crowd." This was a sensationally successful brand strategy at the time. Today, however, we have hundreds of brands that are at least as youthful, hip and fun as Coke. From chocolate cereal bars to sports shoes to coffee, numerous brands are projecting the identical image – the image they believe all consumers have of themselves. The psychographic profile, once a tool for differentiation, has been watered down to a generic formula. Countless products and services are stagnating or losing market share because they are sending the same interchangeable brand image back to the consumer.

In future, brands must evolve from being a mirror to being a megaphone for consumers. The brand's role is now to express something telling which the consumer wants to have expressed. It adds a new, more active aspect to the brand's role. This shift from passive mirror to active megaphone is where we see a major opportunity for tomorrow's brands.

*What* a brand expresses about the consumer is often more important than a factual quality benefit. Indeed, consumers will very likely set aside the better product and go for the brand that lends more *character* – i.e. expresses something about them.

There was a period in the 1980s during which it was cool to wear ripped blue jeans. Rips told stories, like scars on a body, of adventure and a rough, exciting life. Of course, getting your pants ripped at the knee or the seat eventually happened naturally – if you wore them long enough. And if you could not wait that long, you could always use a pair of scissors. Lots of people started doing just that and soon enough the fad caught on to the point that stores began offering "pre-ripped" jeans for sale. There was even a premium kind: they were not just ripped, but had "buckshot wounds." They became a product, a brand in their own right.

The people at Levi's, Lee and all the other manufacturers could only shake their heads at the fact that consumers were willing to pay more for "damaged goods" than for a pair of unscathed, albeit pre-washed, jeans. The rips and gunshot holes, after all, added value: they expressed adventurousness, nonconformism, and, with a little imagination, told a million stories – without the wearer ever having to say a word.

This is just to illustrate how important it is to look *beyond* the product when we look at what we are offering the consumer – and at what the consumer wants the product to tell others.

## THE GROWTH CODES FOR IDENTITY & SELF-EXPRESSION

Developing a successful strategy that makes the brand the megaphone is an option open to products and services in (virtually) all industries. There are, in fact, five growth codes. The right one for your brand will win the consumer's choice and generate higher sales.

1. *Demonstrating character*: In positioning ourselves towards others, we naturally want to emphasize certain character traits – confidence, sophistication, down-to-earthness. We either possess them or we aspire to them. In any case, we want them to be expressed. The brand that successfully – and thus credibly – addresses this need becomes the logical choice. Impressive growth rates have been achieved by applying this principle to products as diverse as beer, a female deodorant, cold medication and a car brand.

2. *Advocating an ideology*: Your brand can take on a deeper role and stand for what your consumer believes in. People feel a need to share their convictions, even to proselytize and convert others to their ideology. The ability to take on this role and vocalize these beliefs can be a compelling purchase argument for your brand. This growth code can achieve success for products ranging from watches to cars.

3. *Attesting kinship*: The group, be it a formal or an informal society, strengthens our individual identity, both to ourselves and to others. We also want the image of our group to rub off on us as its members. This strategy makes your brand a symbol of membership in a special, official or unofficial "society" – one your consumers are proud to belong to or aspire belonging to. The strategies developed for a financial publication and the United States Marine Corps (USMC) illustrate the possibilities.

4. *Creating a hero*: The classic hero, as we know it from literature and Hollywood, is a whole package of enviable and admirable personality traits. A brand, too, can be a heroic personification to the consumer. Here, we look at the mechanics behind creating a hero and learn from movie scriptwriters how these can be applied to a successful brand strategy.

5. *Expressing personal messages*: People use *things* to express something very personal. "Thank you," "I love you," "You are very special to me" – these are messages for which your brand can become the messenger.

These are the five possible tracks to run on after passing through the "Identity and Self-expression" portal in the consumer's mind. As we go into greater detail you will see how a brand strategy can mesh gears with these thought processes and deliver a compelling selling proposition.

## 1. Demonstrating Character

A brand can symbolize a specific, fascinating character trait that the consumer either possesses and/or wishes to demonstrate. It is through the things we do, the choices we make, the brands we buy that others perceive us (or we want others to perceive us) as:

- free, independent
- hip, innovative, trendy
- individualistic/unconventional, interesting
- intelligent
- dependable
- tough, brave, courageous
- having inner strength
- open, tolerant
- laid back, nonchalant
- natural, genuine, down-to-earth
- mature
- clever, astute
- suave, sophisticated
- active, dynamic, sporty
- youthful (in mind) or even
- rebellious, decadent

to name just the obvious ones that spring to mind. But how can your brand become a symbol for one of these character traits? More important, how can it also effectively demonstrate it in a consistent message that will not get garbled along the way? It is not enough to simply assert it about yourself. People who tell us how cool they are instead of *acting* cool just make us roll our eyes.

A brand thus has to *prove* character in order to work as a megaphone. Character, as we know, is something that is mainly expressed through action. Yet it becomes appealing and intriguing to others only when it leads to actions that *diverge from normality*.

Strong personalities stand out by consistently doing the opposite of what most people would do in the same situation. They rise to the occasion when others keep a low profile. And that is what earns them our admiration. This divergence from normality always has a purpose, however.

Here are a few examples.

- Foster's, an Australian beer brand demonstrates "male toughness" as a character trait in marketing its brand in the United States. Here, a huge bush knife is an eloquent symbol of toughness – even more so if it says "Australian for dental floss" underneath the picture. After all, how else would you floss in the Outback? This mechanism makes Foster's appeal to consumers who, were they in a similar situation, would do the same thing with their bush knives – people who feel Foster's expresses (not just reflects) a facet of their own (desired) character.

- Users of Tylenol Flu, a cold medication marketed in the United States, are tougher than the rest. They do not moan and groan when the first flu symptoms appear. Instead, they hang tough, even at the workplace. Where others will stay in bed and nurse themselves back to health, Tylenol Flu users make sure that a cold does not get in the way of getting the job done. The tagline "When the tough get sick" drives home the message about the kind of individual this brand is for.

- Secret, a female deodorant, not only has an extra-strength formula, but also expresses "extra strength" as a character trait. Here, we see a typical Secret user who has just quit a safe job with a big company to start her own business. Her behavior is bold compared with normality – most people *talk* about going into business on their own, but only very few possess the inner strength *to do it*. Here, Secret expresses exactly the strength of character many women aspire to.

The success of these brands comes from their ability to *focus* on a specific character trait, not an overall image of their consumers – and from being a megaphone for their consumers that reinforces both their identity and their self-expression.

Although strong character is mainly demonstrated through action, it is not *exclusively* demonstrated through action. *Any* divergence from normality, even an attitude, has the same effect – as long as there is a discernible purpose behind it. Here are a few examples.

- American shirtmaker Hathaway showed models wearing a black eye patch, which contrasted with conventional associations of sophistication, tradition and style. It expressed an adventurous, dangerous and tough character that rubbed off on consumers and set them apart from the stereotype of the "normal" businessman.

- According to cosmetics brand Marbert, "Every face tells a story." A small scar or blemish does not have to be a flaw: it can even make a face more beautiful and interesting. The Marbert customer is thus very different from all other women who use makeup to *cover up*. The Marbert Woman has character and is proud of it.

It is worth noting here that not only strong characters diverge from normality, but also crazy individuals. Divergence without purpose is simply insanity. Some brands do not make the distinction. A campaign for a mobile telecommunications company, for instance, presents us with a yuppie dangling from a bungee rope and talking on a mobile phone. Another strange character is wearing a suit made of dead fish. Is this the *character* that is supposed to rub off on the consumer?

Where strength of character is a positive divergence from normality and elicits respect and admiration, eccentricity simply attracts attention and catapults you out of the mainstream. Eccentrics make us smile, and they might keep our attention for a while, but we usually do not want to hang around them too much or too long. Again, the key element behind strength of character, when it challenges conventions, is *purpose*.

---

## The Character Principle

*Make your brand the expression of a character trait that your consumers want to express or aspire to possess.*

Success factors:

1. *Link*: The new character trait you choose *should* be derived directly from your brand – ideally from a strength, but possibly also from any interesting aspect of your brand.

2. *Aspiration*: The new character trait you choose must be one your consumers aspire to – and want expressed. Is there anything your consumers perceive as a character deficit that your brand can compensate.

3. *Genuineness*: Your brand must *prove* the character trait it expresses. It is not enough to *state* it. "I'm cool, so you're cool" does not cut it with the consumer in the long run.

4. *Uniqueness*: The more distinctive the new character trait, the more clearly your brand can be differentiated from the competition.

The following example shows how the Character Principle can be a roadmap around seemingly insurmountable marketing obstacles.

## Case in point:  Volvo (Germany)

Volvo was about to launch its new S40 (sedan) and V40 (station wagon) mid-range products and had to solve two major problems. First, how could they break into a market firmly in the hands of Mercedes, BMW and Audi? Secondly, how could they eliminate the stigma of "conservative" that still lingered? Volvo was faced with a very difficult uphill battle.

What Volvo did was to extract a character trait from the brand: it was a small brand compared with its German rivals; it was from a foreign country; it had a distinctive design.

What emerged was a clear character trait: individualism. And market research confirmed that this was also a character trait that a large portion of drivers aspired to.

Thus, the strategy was to make the brand an *expression of individualism*. But how did they *prove* this character trait instead of just asserting "Volvo. The car for individualists."?

Imagine a Volvo V40 speeding up a mountain serpentine. The car stops at the edge of a precipice. The view is breathtaking. The driver steps out, walks over to the edge of the precipice, pulls out a boomerang and tosses it out into the endless valley. He then places an apple on his head and calmly waits for the boomerang to return . . . and slice the apple in half. Our man then leans back against his V40 and takes a bite out of the apple. What makes this man so *individualistic*? It is not only his ability to throw a boomerang – in itself a spectacular feat! It is the self-confidence, discipline, passion and skill that set him apart from millions of "normal" contemporaries. He does not even flinch when the boomerang returns to slice through the apple just inches from his face. This is an *individual-istic* character trait that many German drivers want to possess and express. And only the V40 can project this strength of character on the road. Volvo sales went up 100% within the first year in the mid-size segment.

Audacity is a character trait that motivates individuals to cross the line, to break conventions, rules and laws. They do "the forbidden thing" to achieve their goal. Your brand could be the expression of audacity. How this works is demonstrated by Rolo, a toffee brand from Nestlé.

## Case in point: Rolo (Netherlands)

The confectionery market is probably one of the toughest in the world. Rolo is not only up against other kinds of chocolate-coated caramels, but also competing with sweet drops, gum drops, chocolate bars, marshmallows, and so on. How do you successfully position yet another kind of chocolate toffee in this kind of environment?

What Rolo did was to identify their brand with audacity, a character trait that its young consumers found most appealing. For the brand to express this character in a compelling way, it also had to *prove* how audacious it was. This is how Rolo "crossed the line."

Our hero, a hip teenager, probably a very popular guy at his high school, is sitting in the movie theater. Next to him is a cute girl he just happens to chat up. As part of his spiel, he offers her his last Rolo. The girl is about to pop the toffee into her mouth when along comes this drop-dead blonde who flashes an irresistible smile as she sits down right next to him. We can see from his expression that our hero's mind is racing through the possibilities. "Darn, that was my last Rolo. . . ." is one thought; "It's not too late!" is another: he carefully puts his arm around girl number one's shoulders as if to kiss her, but then grabs her neck and pries the Rolo out of her mouth and offers it to the blonde. The tagline drives home the point: "Think twice about who gets your last Rolo." This outrageous audacity is a character trait many consumers in this age group dream of having – and want to express. Rolo does it for them. Sales doubled within the first year of the campaign.

Character strategies open an inexhaustible source of opportunities for the brand. Find the character trait lodged inside your brand, and create a bridge between it and the character trait your consumers aspire to.

## 2. Advocating an Ideology

Just as *actions* say much about the character of individuals, so do their *beliefs*. Here, the brand is a means of expressing the opinions, convictions, attitudes and ideologies the consumer wants to express. Here are just a few examples of "brand ideologies" that were not only embraced by consumers, but also resulted in market successes.

- "Accept no limits." and "Just do it." (Nike sports shoes and wear)
- "Don't crack under pressure." (Tag Heuer sports watches)
- "Live life to the max." (Pepsi max)

These ideological statements are compelling purchase motivators because they say out loud what their consumers believe in. In a more general sense, ideologies say a lot about the individual: about character, interests, life circumstances and even external features. Just being told that someone is a "Buddhist" or a "feminist" – i.e. stating their ideology – is enough for a certain physical and psychological profile to form in our minds.

But what makes a brand ideology compelling enough to become a purchase motive? The key is *polarization.* In other words, your brand ideology must

- *stand for* a specific ideal and, at the same time,
- *oppose* a prevalent belief, attitude or situation.

Advocating an ideology is always about *challenging* a widely held belief and being unequivocal. This is where most brands fail because they want to stay on the fence and play it safe.

It is precisely the tension from the polarization that creates a coherent, intriguing and credible proposition to the consumer. With the brand as their megaphone, consumers want to communicate something exciting, provoking and true about themselves. To provoke is to polarize.

An ideology that does *not* separate consumers into two camps, i.e. one that anybody and everybody can subscribe to, is a shaky platform for a brand. In Germany, a cigarette brand advocated the ideology of "Come together" – we are all brothers and sisters, regardless of our culture. As noble as this ideology is, it is not compelling as a purchase motive. That is because this ideology is so widely accepted by the mainstream that expressing it is pointless. There is no polarization.

Advocating an ideology means your brand will not only make friends, but also "enemies." This may sound unsettling, but polarization is essential to maximizing the brand opportunity. The important thing is to make sure that whoever's toes you step on are *outside* your target universe. Here are two examples.

- Jeans and apparel brand Diesel took the stodgy establishment head-on. However, since the brand is focused only on serving the youth market it could not care less about alienating older consumers.

- Women's fragrance, Impulse opposed female power against male dominion. Why should Impulse care about men if women are supposed to buy it?

---

## The Ideology Principle

*Power up your brand with a provocative ideology (one clear thought) that your consumers want to proclaim.*

Success factors:

1. *Link*: Take a close look at your product (origin, materials, manufacturing processes and usage) and identify a strength, perhaps even a weakness or a special aspect that could be the platform for an ideology. Example: a particularly robust watch casing is a factual quality that can be translated into an ideology – "robustness" leads to "Don't crack under pressure."

2. *Fascination*: Weigh the possible brand ideologies against each other – which one will *captivate* the consumer? Talk to your consumers and define the nuances of their ideology so that you can be sure of interpreting it correctly.

3. *Polarization*: The ideology you advocate must oppose a prevalent belief, attitude or situation. This polarization is what makes this ideology worth expressing!

4. *Crispness*: A brand ideology is not a long-winded manifesto: it is focused on one absolutely crystal-clear thought.

How can the Ideology Principle be applied in real life? Here is the story of a small Italian car that became a success against overwhelming odds.

## Case in point: Fiat Panda (Germany)

Fiat is losing ground in the small-car segment it used to dominate, slipping from 15.1% to 7.8% of the market. The Japanese are flooding the market with attractive, better-equipped and less expensive models. The Panda is the automaker's "small" big hope to get back on top. The auto press is less than helpful: "A shoebox on wheels . . . and the height of engineering comes in the form of an ashtray you can slide sideways on the dashboard." Compounding the problem, small cars – at least in Germany – all say the same thing about their owners: "I can't afford a real car." What could Fiat possibly do?

Fiat looked at the low weight, low fuel consumption and low profile and distilled it all into a compelling ideology: "I drive a Panda because it's the socially and environmentally responsible thing to do." In other words, being able to afford a "real car" has got nothing to do with it. It is about an ideology.

While owners of big cars are implicitly "not with it" and owners of other small cars exposed as living on the poverty line, Panda drivers are individuals with strong, positive convictions. Market surveys underscored the provocative (polarizing) aspect of the strategy: 75% of the total driving population were completely opposed to the Panda ideology, which only *reaffirmed* the remaining 25% (a large enough universe for the *Panda*). Here are two sample advertisements; you can easily imagine the visuals:

- "Despite an annual salary of DM 250 000 (roughly US$130 000), Mr K sees no need to take more than 700 kg of car to the office."

- "We decided to make the garage a bit smaller and the children's room bigger instead."

This brand ideology made the Fiat Panda the best-selling import in its class, and this despite a below-average marketing budget.

The Ideology Principle lends itself just as effectively to luxury products.

## Case in point: Tag Heuer (International)

Tag Heuer is the fifth largest Swiss watchmaker and markets its products in 90 countries around the world. The company is the acknowledged inventor of the professional sports chronometer. Then again, let us be honest: the circle of individuals who need an extremely shock-resistant, professional sports timepiece – one that, for instance, will not cave in under the pressure of 60 atm – is probably rather small. So how can this special watch capture a larger customer universe?

*Tag Heuer translated the robustness, precision and durability of its watches into the pillars of an ideology: inner strength, focus, endurance.* In other words: "Don't crack under pressure." Think of a tennis player that fends off eight match balls and wins the game against all odds. Tag Heuer then took it a step further: "Success. It's a mind game." Here, the ideology reaches a new extreme. It is about super-achievers who not only win against natural odds, but will also not hesitate to *increase the odds against them*. Whether it is a ballerina doing cartwheels on an I-beam high above the streets of New York, or a track champion running the 100 m hurdle and leaping over giant razor blades – where the natural limits are not high enough, these heros set them higher! This is also where the polarization that is crucial for a successful ideology strategy comes in: Tag Heuer's super-achievers are light-years away from the 99% of the population that consider "difficult" to be difficult enough.

Within two years of the new campaign, Tag Heuer sales were up by an average of 26% throughout Europe, spiking to as much as 72% in some markets.

## 3. Attesting Kinship

Every group projects an image on its members, be it positive, neutral or negative, to outsiders. Picture an individual who would belong to each of the following groups:

- Rotary Club
- Jehovah's Witnesses
- Marine Corps
- New York dance club scene
- Stamp collectors
- Collectors of modern art

Indeed, the name of the group alone is enough to conjure up a pretty clear idea of what its members look like. "Membership" in any of these groups defines a certain outlook or psychological profile. It even defines a physical impression. The ease with which a picture forms in our minds can be disconcerting – and the one you have of the Marine is as clear in your mind as it is different from that of a collector of modern art. If your brand were a membership card, what kind of a club would it be for? Who would be the members of your club?

Keep in mind that a club, by definition, implies certain membership criteria. It appeals to some and not to others. It admits some and rejects others. Before we begin answering these questions and looking at the tools with which to find the answers, let us expound further on the kinds of clubs out there.

A club can also be an *informal society* whose "members" are connected only by certain (statistical) commonalities, for example,

- captains of industry
- geniuses
- yuppies
- ravers
- movie stars

The wealth of special interest magazines, be it for cigar aficionados or mountainbike fans, is an excellent gauge of how large an informal society can be – and how many there are! What the magazine does for the group (validate it), your brand does for the individual member.

Can your brand be a membership card for a social group, an informal society? Find out by mapping your brand against this growth code.

---

### The Membership Principle

*Make your brand the "membership card" of a specific social group or informal society that your consumers are proud to belong to or aspire to belong to.*

Success factors:

1. *Affinity*: There must be an affinity between your brand and the group. Draw up a list of social groups for which your brand would be a natural common denominator.

2. *Group image*: Choose the group on your list your consumer would feel best about belonging to. What

# Penn Bookstore

123105 CASH-1          0262 0314 020

978078790311 TRADE
Treating Sexual Di    MDS 1     35.00
978047172025 TRADE
What Makes Winning    MDS 1     39.95
660 C
NEW TEXTBOOKS         MDS 1N     5.95
     SUBTOTAL           80.90
    7% Sales Tax           5.25
       TOTAL           86.15

APPROVAL: 21
 ACCOUNT NUMBER  3725XXXXXXXXXX 0804
   American Express         86.15
Thank You for Shopping @ Penn Bookstor.

8/03/01  8:49 PM

values, character traits, ideology will membership project onto the consumer? This also must be consistent with your brand.

3. *Focus*: Is there more than one facet to the group's image? Then focus on a point that is particularly relevant to its members – and your brand.

4. *Exclusiveness*: Do you want your brand to raise the (social) status of the group and its members? Demonstrate how exclusive the group is. Look at the prerequisites for membership – what does it take to be a member? Also, if your brand were a person, would it meet these standards?

5. *Credibility*: A plausible, compelling proposition as to why this group or informal society should feel its values are best expressed or embodied by your product.

*Barron's*, an American business magazine, is just one example of how successful a strategy based on the Membership Principle can be.

## Case in point: Barron's (USA)

Barron's is a business weekly, aimed at the affluent investor. The marketing objective was to increase readership, without watering down Barron's upmarket image. Quite a dilemma. The big idea was to see Barron's as a "membership card" for the club of movers and shakers in the financial world. A copy of Barron's tucked under your arm immediately establishes you as a member of that club. The brand communication then built on this idea. A typical ad shows us a high-powered executive reading Barron's. He's sitting behind a barbed-wire fence –

not because he's a prisoner but because he's a well-guarded captain of industry who needs to be insulated from distractions. The headline reads: "Slip past the secretary, the secretary's secretary and the secretary's secretary's secretary. . . ." Between the lines you read, that a subscription to Barron's is the ticket to kinship with the business elite.

The United States Marine Corps uses the same principle, but from a different angle, in a very successful strategy to attract exceptional individuals. . . .

## Case in point: United States Marine Corps (USA)

How does the USMC recruit new people for an officer's career? We already know they have been looking for a few good men for a few decades. But times have changed and a military career lacks the luster of a career on Wall Street. What can the USMC do now to get good people? What are these few good men and women like? They are not adventurers or swashbucklers: Marines are not Legionnaires. The people they want are natural born leaders. The problem is not that there are not enough of them around, but that this rare breed wants to exercise its talents in the business world, not in a military environment.

The big idea here was to build on the compelling proposition of kinship: Being admitted by the marines proves that you are *management material*. One recruitment advertisement read: "Wanted, Company Leaders: Extreme Physical Tests. Demanding mental challenges. Ability to lead under conditions of stress. Few will succeed. Interested? Call 1-800-Marines." Another advertisement: "In many companies it takes years to prove you're management material. We give you 10 weeks." In contrast to business reality, where you start in the mail room, in the marines, you are challenged from day one. – Leads went up 163% and actual recruiting increased by 23%.

## 4. Creating a Hero

A hero personifies *several character traits or virtues* – not just one. A hero is the repository of the qualities we aspire to. You can equip your brand with heroic qualities, that are projected onto the consumer. This you can achieve by applying the same principles Hollywood scriptwriters adhere to in making your brand the hero.

### The Hero Principle

*Make your brand the hero who embodies the sum of character traits your consumer aspires to – by following the same rules that apply in Hollywood.*

Success factors – hero/heroine:

1. *Identification*: Your hero must *not* be an unattainable, elusive idol, but a character that is made from the same stuff as your consumers. They must be able to identify with him. At the same time, the hero is someone the consumer looks up to.

2. *Deficit compensation*: Your hero must compensate for the consumer's (secret) deficits. The hero shows (inner) strength where the consumer suffers from his or her own weakness or insecurity.

3. *Trademark*: Your hero should have a distinctive physical presence. Many film idols (e.g. Charlie Chaplin, Humphrey Bogart) have certain trademarks that make them unforgettable.

4. *Character depth*: Real heroes are not two-dimensional characters. Hollywood scriptwriters believe in weaving a biography for the hero, from childhood to death, before writing the first line of dialogue. Imagine who your brand would be and give substance to the character.

5. *Setting*: The action should take place in a context that is as remote as possible from the consumer's everyday life – a hero has adventures and adventure is escapism. By the same token, an adventure is only as large as the setting in which it unfolds.

Success factors – drama:

What defines a hero is courageous action in the face of extreme (social) situations. This is how a good story begins, unfolds and ends:

1. *A (social) conflict*: Our hero gets into trouble – it is a conflict situation that your consumer can easily picture for him or herself. Example: walking home one evening and being confronted by a hostile street gang.

2. *The victim*: Most often, the hero is the victim of the conflict and then evolves into the character we admire. You might, however, consider giving the victim role to a helpless third party – a pregnant woman, a child or a charming elderly person. In any case, the victim is likeable, innocent and does not stand a chance on his or her own – the hero will save their day.

3. *The foe*: Our hero shines all the more when measured against a menacing foe. The larger, stronger, more powerful or simply detestable the foe, the better. The

foe may be a single individual, a group or an institution.

4. *Resolution*: Our hero will usually resolve the conflict in a head-on confrontation: through cunning, speed, grace and skill. The more original and creative the way our hero handles the situation, the better.

5. *Triumph*: The hero celebrates victory in a noble manner. Triumph can be externalized in lots of different ways: a grateful victim, the recognition of peers, the humiliation of the defeated, etc.

The strict rules of the Hero Principle based on Hollywood standards do not give you a strategic mold for churning out uniform brand concepts. On the contrary, the history of film shows us how incredibly flexible the Hero Principle is. Heroes as different from each other as Tarzan, Superman and James Bond again and again work their magic according to its laws – even Casper the ghost. Or a pair of jeans. . . .

## Case in point: Levi's 501

Levi's 501 are the original Levi's, the "classic" at the origin of a plethora of different styles, cuts and colors. The problem: classic was no longer hip. Levi's was being perceived as losing touch, and getting comfortable. The brand professionals looked at the seven core brand values that made the brand strong – sex, freedom, confidence, rebelliousness, genuineness, youth and "The Original" – and explored the possibilities of bringing them all together. They arrived at a hero strategy. One of the cinema commercials – a hero belongs on the silver screen – for the European market goes as follows.

The scene is set somewhere in the middle of nowhere, deep in the American West, far away from the artificial stress of the modern civilization – a place where a man is a man and only as good as his word. A young fellow with rugged good looks – a drifter, a little rough around the edges – steps into a dim roadside bar. The fat, swarthy bartender challenges him to a game of pool – our hero looks like easy prey. Since our hero does not have any money, the bartender suggests they play for the Levi's our hero is wearing. The suspense mounts as our hero accepts the bet. But he does not look like a pool player at all, much less a hustler. And then it happens: our hero pockets one ball after the other, nonchalantly pointing to the next pocket. He is a natural. And he wins. A heavy silence pours over the dive as the bartender reluctantly pulls out a few greasy bills. Our hero, however, slowly shakes his head, holding the bartender's gaze, and points to the fat man's belt buckle. The bartender, humiliated, gets the drift and drops his pants. Suddenly, the place explodes in hoots and cheers – even the cute barmaid has to bite her lip to keep from laughing. Our hero, oblivious to the applause, simply heads out the door and leaves the bartender to stew on the lesson just learned.

Let us take a look at the ingredients of this application of the Hero Principle. Our hero does not look like an achiever. He is an average, uncomplicated sort of nice guy, nowhere near being a star or a hero. And yet he compensates for a number of deficits on the consumer's side: he is good-looking but in an unobtrusive, self-effacing kind of way; he is laid-back but he is not a push-over; and he lives in a place where life is simple and true, far away from stress, hierarchies and urban fears. More important, he lives in the American West, where everything is big and adventure still exists – a place that has lost nothing of its fascinating mystique and never will. And to recap how the story follows the dramaturgical laws of a Hollywood production:

1. *(Social) conflict:* The plan is to humiliate our hero in front of the roughnecks in the bar. There is no escape: he is a wimp if he refuses to play and he is a wimp if he loses. And at first it also looks like he cannot win.

2. *The victim* is our hero. He is obviously innocent, being bullied and that is how he immediately wins our support.

3. *The foe* is personified by the fat greasy bartender who represents the complacent, pushy grownup world. Defeating him proves a lot more than being a good pool player.

4. *Conflict resolution:* Our hero wins through superior skill. He displays quiet strength. He wins and makes his point. He also shows strength of character – making a point is more important than money (which he could obviously use). He will not kick a man lying on the ground, but he will not let him off the hook either.

5. *The triumph:* The bartender has to drop his pants. Ironically, the people he tried to impress are now making fun of him. Even the barmaid, his employee, suppresses a laugh. Our hero, however, does not hang around to be celebrated. He is just a cool dude who does not let anybody step on his toes.

In the three-year period in which this cinema campaign hit the screens across Europe, Levi's market share increased between 36% and 88% in various European markets.

So far, we have described four growth codes on which to build a solid brand strategy with that area of the consumer's mind that deals with Identity & Self-expression. There is one important aspect of self-expression, however, that we have not covered so far. It deals with our interactions with others. Here we will see how a brand can become the medium for expressing a more personal facet of our character.

## 5. Expressing Personal Messages

Your brand can also act as a messenger to others – and amplify the message you are sending. People have been saying it with flowers ever since time can remember. The choice of flower makes the message as general or as specific as you want it to be:

- Red roses: "I love you."
- White carnation: "I'm still available."
- Narcissus: "You're vain."
- Columbines: "I think you're a wimp."
- Edelweiss: "Your beauty overwhelms me."
- Georgina: "I'm already taken."
- Geraniums: "I'll be waiting for you at our favorite spot."
- Chestnut blossoms: "Can you forgive me?"
- Crocus: "I need time to think it over."
- Mallow: "You're as cold as ice."
- Rosemary: "I've given up on you."
- Hemlock: "You betrayed me."

Keep these in mind the next time you are in the flower shop wondering what kind of bouquet to send. In Australia, for instance, there is a flower shop that will deliver a neatly wrapped bouquet of wilted roses to a special someone in your life that has done you a bad turn. Yes, you can say *that* too with roses.

A specific brand, like a specific flower, can be an effective messenger. Chocolates, sweets, liquor and toys are obvious candidates for expressing a personal message. The key is to claim a particular occasion or message for your brand, and your brand alone. Once your brand is established as the messenger of choice, it can even override a qualitative advantage your competitors may have.

---

## The Messenger Principle

*Make your brand synonymous with an important personal message consumers want to send to others.*

Success factors:

1. *Suitability*: The Messenger Principle works best for products or services that play an important role in social interactions, such as gifts to show esteem, respect, love, gratitude.

2. *Significance*: The message should be as important as possible – no banalities.

3. *Frequency*: Your message should be one that is sent *frequently* by your consumer. Can your product be an effective, genuine way of expressing "Thank you!", "I think you're wonderful," or "You're very special."? These are only the most obvious occasions – be creative!

---

Cadbury's Roses, a British chocolate brand, positioned itself as a small, informal everyday gift. "Say it with roses" is the simple and crystal-clear message that struck a chord with consumers. The brand quickly surpassed Quality Street, the leading gift chocolate brand – even though Quality Street had more than twice the market share and had a significantly higher marketing budget. The Messenger Principle is just as effective for big-ticket items. . . .

## Case in point: De Beers Diamonds (International)

How do we market diamonds to consumers at the beginning of a world-wide recession? Not as an investment, but as a luxury item. The challenge seems impossible if we take a closer look at what we are up against:

1. Diamonds are *per se* the *opposite* of a brand – each one is unique. No two diamonds are alike in terms of quality, origin, price and packaging.

2. The positioning has to work in 23 countries: from the United States to Saudi Arabia; from Thailand to Japan – this in view of the fact that diamonds have a different traditional and cultural significance from country to country. People buy one for different reasons and on different occasions.

3. Diamonds and diamond jewelry have no *practical* value to the consumer – this makes them even more sensitive to a recession than other luxury products, e.g. timepieces.

4. The spectrum of competitors is broad and deep. From the consumer's perspective, a diamond is a major investment and in the same category as a (family) vacation, a major household appliance, a mortgage payment, etc. Compounding the problem, today's technology makes synthetic diamonds virtually indistinguishable from the real thing and much more affordable.

5. De Beers is willing to invest 4% of turnover in marketing, where other luxury goods brands normally invest three to six times as much.

Where can a strategy even begin to define a lever for generating more sales? A number of sales arguments are close at hand: perfection in quality, immaculate beauty, indestructability and timeless value. But these are rather "cold" product benefits and they quickly become irrelevant in the face of higher financial priorities and concerns in a recessive economy. De Beers solved the problem by making diamonds the "ultimate message of love". Love is something everyone on this planet can respond to – as a giver and as a recipient. And what better way to express one's undying love for someone than with something that is also eternal? After all, "A diamond is forever." Here, the preciousness, exorbitant price and unique value of a diamond is reduced to one single message: "I love you." The diamond proves that the love it symbolizes is total and eternal. And the substantial cost of a diamond – especially during a recession – actually reinforces the message. The De Beers strategy delivered astonishing results. Some markets reported a sales increase in the 20% to 25% range. In the United States alone, the campaign generated US$2.7 billion in new sales. All with a global marketing budget of just US$113 million.

## SUMMARY

Brands are a uniquely effective means of defining and expressing the consumer's identity. They are like colors on a painting palette. The consumer is the artist and uses them to create the different shades and hues of his or her own character. Brands can proclaim the consumer's character as well. They are a means of positioning consumers in a social context. In this sense, the brand can take the responsibility for making certain things clear about the consumer: "I am successful." – "I am a pacifist." – "I am an intellectual." – "I am hip." – "I am a Christian." – "I am a rebel." – these are all statements of character that a brand can successfully communicate.

There is nothing a specific brand could not express about its user, owner, wearer. Check the different ways in which your brand can proclaim your consumer's identity in terms of

1. Demonstrating character

2. Advocating an ideology

3. Attesting kinship

4. Creating a hero

5. Expressing personal messages

One thing is for sure in all cases: the consumer is not keen on expressing anything boring or conventional about him or herself. Find out the single most important message your consumer would like to share with the world – be it about him or herself or what he or she believes in. Almost any product or service in any industry can profit from these brand strategies: cars, fashion brands, jewelry even personal care products.

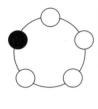

# Portal 5: Emotions & Love

**Premise**: *Consumers prefer your product or service because they "love" the brand.*

Love happens in private life, but also, as we will see, in the supermarket when we buy certain things instead of others. It is out of love for other people that we make unselfish gifts, make sacrifices and put our own interests on the back seat – for the sake of a companion, children, parents or friends. To act out of love is to act without expecting anything in return – except perhaps a little love. Just how far love can go is demonstrated by the historic decision taken by King Edward VIII of the United Kingdom who abdicated his throne for the love of commoner Wallis Simpson. In this chapter we will show that the consumer also loves certain brands, and that these brands are loved with such intensity that the consumer will remain loyal to them for a lifetime. How can a brand generate such intense feelings? Here, too, our research yielded growth codes, which are applicable to all industries. Let us now enter the fifth portal in the consumer's mind. It is all about big emotions.

## ABOUT THE LOVE FOR *THINGS*

As strange as it may sound, loving objects, inanimate things, is something we do readily. The neighbor "loves" his car, the child loves its teddy bear, and your girlfriend loves her favorite sweater. Some objects conjure up sweet feelings when we see them or touch them. They serve as repositories of emotions. Mementos fulfill the function of conserving the memories we have of people, places or events. They rarely offer a *practical* use.

The love children have for their dolls or teddy bears is especially strong. They develop the same kind of emotional bond with objects as they do with people. Little girls speak with their dolls, feed them, care for them, and even administer "medical treatment" in case of an "injury." And when the doll breaks or gets damaged, funerary ceremonies are quite in order. Grownups love objects, too. *"Das Auto ist des Deutschen liebstes Kind* – 'the car is the German's dearest child'," the saying goes. And it is not only true in Germany. People all over the world give their car a name, whisper sweet nothings and gently stroke the dash when it does not behave as it should.

The Tamagochi craze is another expression of the phenomenon. Japanese computer game manufacturer Bandai created a little egg-shaped electronic pet the size of a keychain fob: the game is to raise it from cradle to grave. Press a button and a little virtual chick is born on an LCD display. It needs to be cared for and nurtured. Little beeps remind the owner to feed, clean, wash and tell a bedtime story, all by pressing a button. Neglect translates into a grouchy Tamagochi that becomes moody and a real pain. No care at all and the creature starves and dies. Within six months, more than 13 million of these US$20 surrogate babies were sold worldwide. School kids became so engrossed that the craze disrupted the classroom. Very soon, schools began to officially ban the toy. In Tokyo, commuters passed time taking care of their electronic friend. Help lines were set up and advice columns appeared on how best to care for your Tamagochi. Even Internet sites were created, with graveyards for dear departed ones. Developing very strong love ties with objects is something we humans find very easy to do. With brands, too.

There is no expiration date on feelings. Once an object is infused with emotions, they merge with it and become part of a whole. Let us suppose you own an old worn-down baseball cap. It is a memento of a bygone romance. Woven into every fiber are lots of passionate memories that simply will never wash out. Emotions are like a seductive fragrance that always lingers around the object. The feeling is just as much part of the baseball cap as it is of any other object. The thing is, it is the feelings and emotions that make the object so valuable, so irreplaceable and precious. Just imagine if someone picked the old cap off the chair and tossed it into the garbage can. No doubt that person would think they had done you a favor. But how would you feel? A new cap would not mean anything to you. Physical quality is no longer an issue when love is in play. *Quality alone cannot replace the emotional value of an object* – love is always something exclusive, unique, while quality is easily reproducible. We love no person the same way we do another. The same applies to the love we develop for brands.

## THE QUANTUM LEAP FROM "LIKE" TO "LOVE"

Emotions sell. So, what else is new? Strangely enough, there are countless brands out there that (ab)use emotions to plug their products and still fail. That is because they arouse too weak an emotional response. They are content with sympathy, or with being liked. The problem is that "like" is not an exclusive feeling. The consumer might find your product just as likeable as that of competitors A, B or C. And that is why the consumer flits from one brand to another, liking one a little more one day and a little less the other, depending probably on which one is on sale.

"Like" is not enough. You want love. Only then will the consumer stay true to you, in good times and bad, even when the competition waves a big "sale" sign in front of the consumer. This emotional tie is what we call brand bonding. It can be achieved with growth codes that can be applied to virtually any product or service, even toilet paper.

## HOW DO YOU MAKE LOVE HAPPEN?

Loyalty is what defines the quantum leap from "like" to "love." But what *practical* or *methodical* consequences result from it? Brand professionals do not need a new method for making people *like* the brand, but they do need one to create *love*. How does love "work"? Scientists have been trying to get behind the "rules" of love. When does someone fall in love with someone else – and why? Stendhal, a nineteenth century French novelist, made some remarkable observations of the French court long before psychology even had a name. Theses such as "One falls more easily in love with that which is individual, exclusive and unique" or "That which is genuine elicits more love than what seems artificial" ring as true today as they did then and as they will a thousand years from now. A feeling of love can be stored in, for instance, a scent, a melody or in the memory of a special situation. However, to find out how to create love for a brand, we need more precise guidelines. Winning brands that have succeeded in making themselves loved instead of just well liked show us the way.

# THE GROWTH CODES FOR EMOTIONS & LOVE

Understanding how love works is a major challenge. Before we get into the nuts and bolts, let us first differentiate between a number of fundamental approaches to eliciting "brand bonding."

1. *Being a friend*: Showing solidarity is a way for your brand to be much more to your consumers than a product or service. If your consumers feel deluded, misunderstood or rejected by others or society – your brand can stand by them and "fight a common enemy." Invest in friendship with your consumers and you can be sure of their loyalty.

2. *Tapping into emotions*: The consumer's mind is full of emotions that are connected to experiences, memories and notions. We call them emotional nodes. The love of one's country, for instance, is such a node. It can be tapped and fused with your brand. This works much faster and more effectively than building a love relationship from scratch.

3. *Nurturing a yearning*: People yearn for romance, a dream vacation or a life away from it all in the countryside, for instance. Brands can come to epitomize these yearnings without having to deliver *fulfillment*. The yearning itself, triggered by the brand, become the compelling purchase motive.

4. *Arousing empathy*: Your brand can be the originator of emotional stories consumers will empathize with and credit you for. This principle builds on the techniques applied by masters in the art of storytelling. The reason millions of readers buy their best sellers is because they love the stories. Your brand can be loved for the same reason.

## 1. Being a Friend

What makes a friend? A friend is someone who understands us, especially at those points where others do not understand us. A friend comes to our defense even when we make mistakes. True friendship is about solidarity that does not shine through in the smooth, happy-go-lucky routines of everyday life, but when the going gets tough.

A brand can show solidarity just as a friend does, in a variety of ways.

- It can publicly defend the unpopular beliefs of its consumers (e.g. for kids: "I hate school!")
- It can boost the self-confidence of its users (e.g. gays and lesbians)
- It can attack social inequities that worry consumers (e.g. unemployment)
- It can publicly go against "enemies" of consumers (e.g. the fans of the opposing football team)

Taking sides with the consumer creates a stronger bond than a "like" feeling. You want the consumer to love your brand – because that makes it more difficult to philander.

So, how do you demonstrate solidarity? Try to find an *emotional issue* in your consumer's life that preoccupies him or her more than others. It must be an issue that is either ignored, not understood or even rejected by peers. Any emotional conflict offers the opportunity to show solidarity with consumers – and they are receptive to it.

---

### The Solidarity Principle

*Position your brand as an ally to your consumers on one important emotional issue that other people ignore, do not understand or deny.*

---

Success factors:

1. *Emotional issue*: The issue on which your brand becomes the consumer's ally must have a high emotional intensity. Search for the role in which your brand can show solidarity and be a friend. Build a bridge between your brand and that emotion.

2. *Common enemy*: Your brand should make a stand against the "enemy" who does not understand your consumer. A common enemy can often create the strongest bond.

3. *Genuineness*: It is not enough to just *say* that you are a good friend. *Prove* it by openly taking sides with your consumer. And walk the talk.

Here are three examples to show the scope of solidarity:

- A moisturizer brand addressed the feeling of neglect experienced by the 50+ set (the emotional issue), and established age and maturity as being admirable (solidarity).

- An office supplies franchise attracts kids, who hate school and feel patronized by grown-ups (the emotional issue). The brand became their friend by encouraging their mischievous rebelliousness (solidarity).

- A tabloid paper increased its readership among the larger public, who feel powerless in the rat race (the emotional issue). The brand adopts the role of the people's advocate by poking fun at the ruling class (solidarity).

In real marketing life, the Solidarity Principle can help overcome the toughest challenges. The Nike sports brand demonstrates it aptly . . .

## Case in point: Nike (USA)

Skateboarders are probably the most cynical bunch of consumers around, and many were suspicious if not downright hostile to the idea of Nike entering their domain. Being megabig made Nike uncool. Regardless of their quality, Nike products suffered from the simple fact of being from Nike. Before even contemplating skateboarders as a market, the brand had to overcome this huge aversion. But how? Market research showed there was a powerful *emotional issue* at work with skateboarders: they felt ostracized, disrespected and treated like criminals by society. Here is where Nike could take a stand and be their ally.

The brand publicly raised the question "What if we treated all athletes the way we treat skateboarders?" Who would curse and yell at a jogger the way people do at skateboarders? Who would imagine cops chasing a tennis player across town at night the way they charge after skateboarders? What law enforcement agent would confiscate a golfer's clubs and threaten him with a fine and jail? Nike conjured up these absurd scenarios to *prove* that Nike knew skateboarders, understood them and had the guts to defend them.

## 2. Tapping Into Emotions

Here is another way of charging up your brand with emotions so powerful that they become a purchase motive: by tapping into emotions that are already stored in the consumer's mind. But how does that work? Are emotions not nebulous, fuzzy, there one minute and gone the next? True, but when they connect with memories, experiences and notions, they suddenly become more tangible, more durable. They crystallize into something we call an *emotional node*. A romantic emotion is a fuzzy feeling, but when it connects to a specific childhood memory, a movie or a holiday experience, it crystallizes into what we call an emotional node.

How emotional nodes form in our minds is best explained by an analogy. Pour a little salt into a full glass of water and watch the salt crystals quickly dissolve. The salt is still present in the water, but it is everywhere – and nowhere. It is the same with emotions that flit around in our minds, never staying in place. Drop a thread into the water, however, and gradually you will see the salt bond to the thread and crystallize into a solid, tangible structure. Feelings and emotions act in the same way as they attach themselves to a memory, an experience or a notion and create an emotional node.

Most of the time, these emotional nodes are tucked away deep in our minds, waiting to be activated by a word or an image. Patriotism is a good example. Latent most of the time, this emotional node unleashes overwhelming feelings when the national soccer team wins the world championship. Millions jump out of their chairs in front of the TV and run down into the streets to start hugging perfect strangers.

How emotional nodes fuse with objects – and thus with brands – becomes clear when we think of mementos. Imagine finding a trinket received long ago from a former companion. It stimulates a powerful emotional node and it resonates with romantic memories. The emotional node it is fused with makes the trinket precious – unless, of course, similarly strong emotions motivate you to throw the damn thing out the window! Not only can an object be infused with an *emotional* value, but that value can also be greater than the *material* value. This is the opportunity you can seize for your brand.

---

**The Emotional Node Principle**

*Stimulate an existing "emotional node" in your consumer's mind and fuse it with your brand.*

Success factors:

1. *Link*: Your brand must connect with an existing emotional node stored in the consumer's mind (e.g. patriotic feelings).
2. *Intensity*: The emotional node your brand is connecting with must have intensity – it must elicit a meaningful emotional response.
3. *Genuineness*: Feelings are *always* individual and original – they are *personal*. It is also in the nature of "big feelings" *not to be perfect*. Think about how a stammer in a declaration of love is much more compelling than smoothly delivered poetry.

---

The Emotional Node Principle is also at the core of a very effective marketing tool: merchandising. The idea is to fuse the emotional mode created by a movie (e.g. a Walt Disney movie and its characters) with your own brand. Suddenly, objects that had no personality whatsoever come alive – like lunch boxes and book bags. The license to make these kinds of products part of the world of *Jurassic Park*, *Beauty and the Beast* or *Star Wars* is a license to link up with an emotional node and equip your brand with a powerful purchase motive.

How this growth code can not only take your brand out of a marketing impasse, but also set it on a course for new growth is illustrated by the following example from the tobacco industry.

## Case in point: f6 (Germany)

f6 is a very well-established cigarette brand from Dresden (former East Germany). A market leader before the Berlin Wall came crashing down, the brand went into a downward spiral when the two Germanys were reunited: the effect of instant westernization was that nobody wanted to buy East German brands anymore. More than four decades of knowing what was on supermarket shelves just a few hundred feet away but never being able to buy it had created a tremendous vacuum. Anything "made in the West" was simply better – including cigarettes. The sense of country, of belonging to a specific cultural set, was turned upside down – as was the sense of loyalty to products made at home. Only after years has the craze for things western begun to subside. This was the big opportunity for f6: to tap into *patriotism* and fuse it with the brand. On huge outdoor billboards and print advertisements they proudly presented nothing but the product and a headline, e.g. "Our number one." "The original from Dresden." "Our own classic." "This one or none." The common thread was that all these advertisements had the same core message: forget about all those western cigarette brands – this one is *your* brand. A brand from around here for the people who live around here. All quality and flavor arguments turn out to be so petty and insignificant when it is about country and home. Within 12 months, f6 increased its market share from 15% to 32%, making it the third biggest cigarette brand in reunified Germany.

Identifying the right emotional node can make your brand the logical choice in a very important human event as well. . . .

## Case in point: Warner–Lambert EPT (USA)

How would you market an early pregnancy test (EPT)? The only really important purchase decision should be the reliability of the test, should it not? And that is the problem: they all have the same high degree of accuracy. So what could be a stronger purchase motive for EPT? Let us step back and look at the emotional environment. The moment between "Yes" and "No" almost has unbearable tension. Which situations in life can possibly be more charged with emotion – than the moment that marks a turning point in the life of a couple. Warner–Lambert tapped into this moment: *the intense happiness when anticipation becomes reality* is an emotional node that becomes fused with the brand. The result is a powerful purchase motive in the minds of young couples who find themselves in this situation.

A look at the creative execution takes us into the home of a young, attractive and appealing couple – these are not actors, but real people in a real situation. She has just taken the test and they are both waiting for the result. The sense of anticipation is almost palpable. Now the test is complete and we know for sure: the test is positive, they are going to have a baby. Tenderly, the man presses his companion to his chest and kisses her hair. "I knew it," he whispers. "Congratulations. Are you happy?" That is how the brand fuses with the emotional node of the moment – and become the logical choice in the eyes of the consumer.

There are also emotional nodes which are completely independent of memories, experiences and notions – we are born with them. Think of the emotions that start flowing at the sight of a newborn baby, a cute puppy or a sensual body. . . . Even if these feelings are just a biological reflex, they, too, can be fused with a brand.

## Case in point: Andrex (UK)

Is the kind of toilet paper you use important to you? Most people in Europe are perfectly satisfied with the best deal that is on sale at the moment. One amazing exception is the British Andrex brand. It is between 20% and 50% more expensive than competing toilet paper brands and yet it consistently maintains more than 30% of the British market. The key to the success of Andrex: an irresistibly cute golden Labrador puppy. For more than two decades, this little dog has been taking Andrex from strength to strength. That is because the natural, instinctive love we feel for a cute little puppy dog (the emotional node) was successfully fused with the brand. The puppy has become one with the brand: Since people love the puppy, they love the brand. It can be that simple.

## 3. Nurturing a Yearning

Whereas tapping into emotions involves memories, a yearning is wishful thinking about what could be. It can be a fantasy, the dream of a perfect life, the idea of leaving it all behind. . . . Before we explore the possibilities any further, let us discuss a few insights. First, *you cannot invent a yearning*. The most powerful yearnings are those that have been and will be dreamt a million times. In other words, they already exist and they are already emotionally charged in the consumer's mind. *Discover* them. Secondly, *at the beginning of any yearning there is deprivation*. Yearnings only surface when you are missing something in your life. Conversely, if you are perfectly content you will not experience any yearnings. Freedom, for instance, is something a free individual takes for granted – no big emotions here. But for a prisoner, there is no greater yearning than that for freedom – because it is what he *misses most*. Thirdly, *a yearning reaches its climax at the point of turning into gratification*. If our prisoner is released, he will never enjoy his freedom as much as he did on that very first day. Think about how much you enjoy the first day of spring after a long, harsh winter. Just wait a week and that first springtime feeling is already a little less intense; after a month that first intense rush has already completely faded.

A brand that epitomizes a yearning enjoys the same strong love as the yearning itself. By nurturing a yearning, by making it come alive in the imagination in all its fascinating detail, your brand can close the distance between individuals and their fantasies. The good news is that just because your brand stands for a yearning, it does not mean it has to fulfill it. The yearning is a purpose in *itself*.

The spectrum of possible yearnings is broad indeed. In this chapter we will focus on one very specific variant; namely, the yearning for the ideal lifestyle.

## The Lifestyle Principle

*Make your brand the window into an ideal lifestyle your consumers yearn for.*

Success factors:

1. *Yearning potential:* The lifestyle you choose is one that consumers already yearn for – you only need to discover it and own it for your brand. Do not choose an original lifestyle for the sake of originality or trendiness – it may not be charged with emotions, yet.

2. *Authenticity:* The ideal world in the mind of your consumers is a hazy place, nebulous. Fill in the blanks, make it real. Show this world from morning to night, in all phases of the year, in all its fascinating details.

This shortens the distance between consumers and their yearnings.

3. *Archetypes*: The characters in this ideal lifestyle setting only have the function of populating it: they are archetypes, *not* heroes. For all intents and purposes, the consumer is the hero – he or she may not be upstaged.

4. *Non-drama*: Every moment, every routine is intriguing – there is no *need* for drama. Dramatic episodes would only distract consumers from the essence of the lifestyle.

5. *Location*: The lifestyle must be "home" somewhere. Consumers should have the feeling that they could get there if they wanted to. Give your consumers a rough idea of where on a map this ideal life could be happening. Give that "home" a name.

6. *Mission*: An ideal life always has a purpose. It is not just about fun and games. It is *not* about fleeing responsibilities. It is about defining an ideal environment that is populated by individuals with a purpose – this may be the simple purpose of making a living.

7. *Security*: Your consumers' real lives are full of uncertainties. The ideal life should therefore be as free of them as possible. This entails . . .

   • *Independence*: There is no hierarchy, no dependency, no competition. Roles and activities are clearly defined.

- *Contained setting*: It is a safe haven, an enclave. There is no traffic between the real world and the ideal world.
- *Controlled destiny*: There is no tragedy, no danger or accident, no illness, injuries, disasters or deaths.
- *Timelessness*: There is no beginning and no end. There are no clocks ticking – anything that is set in a timeframe would only destabilize the dream.

8. *Grittiness*: Eternal sunshine and fun in the sun is not what people ultimately yearn for. The true excitement of life is in the interplay between hardship and reward. Hardship is what makes reward fulfilling. Love in the haystack is much more romantic than in a designer penthouse suite. Likewise, a sudden rain shower while walking on the beach. The perfect life is not about everything being perfect – it is the imperfections that make it perfect.

No brand exemplifies the lifestyle principle as aptly and completely as Marlboro. Let us take a look behind the scenes . . .

### Case in point: Marlboro (Worldwide)

Why is Marlboro so successful? Here we have to set aside the nature of the product and its addictive qualities and the fact that this makes

Marlboro equal to any other cigarette brand. It is not just quality because other cigarettes taste just as good – in fact, in blindfold tests, Marlboro smokers may not recognize their own brand. Marlboro's success resides in the brand's ability to nurture yearnings. (The other cornerstone of the brand's success is its ability to express character traits consumers aspire to. Consumers can express "cowboy qualities": maturity, manliness, genuineness. . . .) Let us now map the cowboy world against the success factors of the Lifestyle Principle.

1. *Yearning potential*: Marlboro did not invent the cowboy world – it was already established through decades of westerns and emotionally charged with a romantic vision of the Far West.

2. *Authenticity*: The Marlboro Country is so "real" it feels like you could hop into a plane and fly there. How do they do it? Three things:

   • *Genuineness:* Marlboro makes no compromises in portraying this lifestyle. The cowboys in it are real men, not blow-dried and manicured models. The people we see live there "for real".

   • *Continuum:* The Marlboro Country has a full day, four seasons, good weather and bad. The "completeness" of time is what makes it real.

   • *Detail:* The fact that the consumer has a diffuse idea of what his or her ideal world would look like is precisely what makes a detailed setting more effective. From the worn-out cowboy boots to the lizard slithering behind a rock – every detail makes Marlboro Country more real and believable.

3. *Archetypes*: The Marlboro cowboys are just cowboys, nothing more and nothing less. As archetypes their role is to stand for a lifestyle

– that's *all*. For these cowboys, there is no before, no after and no existence outside Marlboro Country. They have no right to a name, a private life, personal traits or idiosyncrasies. We do not know anything about them and we do not really want to, either. By creating a character and giving it depth, we risk upstaging the consumer in his or her ideal lifestyle. A hero, like John Wayne, would steal the scene.

4. *Non-Drama*: Marlboro Country is free of dramatic stories. We only see cyclical, everyday routines that happen in their own natural rhythm.

5. *Location*: Everybody knows where cowboys live – they live in Marlboro Country. And we have a pretty clear idea of where this place is, somewhere in the American West.

6. *Mission*: Marlboro cowboys are just doing their job and making a living. They are not vacationers or social dropouts. They fulfill a simple but important mission: taking care of the herd.

7. *Security*: The cowboy lifestyle suggests precisely the kind of security and stability the consumer misses in his or her *own* life. There is no talk about divorce, downsizing, social security. . . . But what else is there that makes the Marlboro Country so safe and so secure? Four things:

   • *Independence*: We experience cowboys who are not dependent on anything or anyone. They live off the land, need little technology to sustain themselves and it is of the simplest kind.

   • *Contained setting*: The cowboys do not leave their territory. They are not interested in a trip to another place, to New York or elsewhere. Likewise, there are no strangers who come to visit.

- *Controlled destiny*: Nothing happens that could disrupt Marlboro Country routines. No disasters, no disease, no death.
- *Timelessness*: There is no sense of aging, evolution or progress. It is always the same old coffeepot on the campfire.

8. *Grittiness*: Our cowboys work hard during the day, come rain or shine. Their reward is a wholesome meal with true friends by the campfire. Roughing it is part of the irresistible down-to-earth charm of Marlboro Country.

As soft and fuzzy the world of emotions is, a number of strict rules need to be observed if you want your brand to grow in it. An ideal lifestyle inspires and captures our imagination all the more effectively by adhering to precisely defined success factors. Making the Lifestyle Principle work for your brand requires focus, discipline and uncompromising attention to detail.

## 4. Arousing Empathy

The strategies described so far build on the emotional potential *already* anchored in the consumer's mind. We are now going to *create* this potential. Here, we focus on is the ability of best-selling authors to arouse emotions so powerful that people *love* their books – and that is what makes them loyal customers. There are winning brands out there that are telling similar stories and enjoying unparalleled growth. Why? Because these brands create and maximize emotions the same way master storytellers do: through *empathy*.

## The Empathy Principle

*Make your brand a master storyteller by arousing and maximizing empathy. Let the brand set the tone.*

Success factors:

1. *Hero*: Empathy requires a hero/heroine. Not a cliché character, but an individual appearance. Our hero is not a muscle-bound superhuman, but rather a lovable, vulnerable person who may even appeal to the paternal and maternal instincts of the consumer.

2. *Frustration*: Our lovable hero/heroine is sad or unhappy – either fate has dealt an unfortunate hand or he or she has been the victim of injustice. Whatever happened, he or she has been wronged and is innocent.

3. *Turning point*: Something surprising happens and gives the story a happy twist. This is also where the brand comes in. The hero's unhappiness turns into happiness.

4. *Happy end*: Our hero is overjoyed and shows it in his or her own very special way. The mood swing is so strong that it deeply moves the consumer.

These simple rules of drama give you plenty of room to maneuver. After all, even after thousands of stories, novelists still manage to conceive new and compelling stories according to these set rules. The most telling example of how successfully this approach can be applied to brand marketing is Barilla, an Italian pasta brand.

## Case in point: Barilla (Italy)

How do you even begin to market pasta in Italy, with 400 brands competing for market share – and hope to make a difference? Quality is a given, shots of steaming, delicious-looking pasta on a plate have been done and redone *ad nauseam*. . . . There was nothing Barilla could tell consumers about its brand or its product that they did not already know. So where could there possibly be a purchase motive? Barilla succeeded in creating an emotional bond with the consumer that was so strong that it transcended any marketing issues and still made the brand the logical choice. Barilla became a master storyteller.

Imagine a cute little boy standing in front of the huge gate of a soccer stadium. We can hear the cheering and the foghorns – a major game is under way. Our little hero is sadly staring up at the closed gate – he does not have enough money for a ticket. The streets are swept empty, everybody is either in the stadium or watching the game on TV. There he is, our little boy, sitting on a bench opposite the big gate. So close, but yet so far – he can only listen to the game on his little pocket transistor radio. Suddenly, the box office teller, an old man, waves at him, waves him over, in fact. Our hero is a bit incredulous, the old man cannot possibly be meaning him. The man waves again, encouraging the boy to come over. Hesitantly, the youngster walks up to the old man who flashes a warm smile. He opens the gate just a crack and with a conspiring wink he gently nudges the boy into the stadium. Emotions climax as we see our young hero leaping up the stairs towards the cheering crowd. Just before he reaches the top, he turns around, beaming with a grateful smile. The sparkle in his eyes tells us all we want to know.

This little story picks up on the success factors of maximizing empathy:

- An innocent, lovable hero
- He is very sad and not responsible for the sadness
- A good soul comes to the rescue
- Deep sadness is transformed into huge bliss

Barilla tells a whole series of these stories, all under the motto, "Home is where Barilla is." And what about the noodles? Creating an emotional story does not necessarily require the product to have a part in it, but the brand to be the master storyteller. This approach helped Barilla grow 35% within three years against overwhelming odds.

## SUMMARY

Growth codes exist that can systematically arouse strong emotions that will determine consumer choice to the benefit of your brand. But it is not enough to get consumers to "like" your brand. You want them to *love* it. Because love is the only exclusive feeling that leads to true, unwavering loyalty – that is at the core of brand growth. But how do we even start to talk about love. Think about . . .

- Being a friend
- Tapping into emotions
- Nurturing a yearning
- Arousing empathy

This is not about making an emotional *promise* that your brand has to deliver on (these strategies were discussed in Benefits & Promises). It is about dousing your brand with a special emotional pheromone that will irresistibly draw consumers to it.

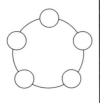

# Working with Growth Codes

Now that you are more familiar with the five portals into the consumer's mind and the growth codes that determine brand success, let us recap the main arguments for working with them – and put them to the test. As you have seen, these growth codes are not only unique but also universal – they can be applied to all products and services in all industries and in all markets regardless of culture, momentary trends and new market developments. That is because the blw method works very much like an equation in mathematics. Each growth code is an equation for increased sales and market share: the formula never changes, only the variables. Before we look at ways of applying growth codes to solving marketing challenges, let us first summarize how they will in fact simplify the task for brand professionals.

## WHAT GROWTH CODES CAN DO FOR YOU

Here are the six key thoughts:

1. *Every growth code opens a universe*: Growth codes do not confine but broaden creativity. They are not off-the-shelf panaceas but a means for developing brand strategies spe-

cifically tailored to your product, market and situation. One single growth code can be the seed to success for countless products or services in any industry, over and over again. Growth codes challenge you to think outside the box and explore viable new strategic options. As you become more adept at applying them, growth codes will enable you to approach marketing opportunities from a broader and deeper perspective, and much more quickly and efficiently than before. You will discover possibilities no one ever considered in all the time you have been marketing your product or service.

2. *Growth codes have no expiration date*: Growth codes are distilled from *past* experience, which begs the question whether they can be the basis for something completely new and innovative in the *future*. Yes, they can! Although we may look a thousand years into the future and discover that brands look quite different from today, one constant will still hold true: every brand depends on addressing a compelling purchase motivation. The brand still has to click with the consumer. Growth codes will not expire or become obsolete. They can only be expanded, supplemented and refined.

3. *From growth codes to supercodes*: Since thinking in growth codes also opens new ways to interpret your brand, your market and your consumer, new thought structures will emerge. The more comfortable you are handling the various growth codes, the easier it will be to establish connections between them. Several growth codes can be networked to address all the facets of a marketing challenge, and the resulting *supercode* will give your brand an even stronger foundation for new growth. Riding these growth code interchanges

will accelerate the strategic development process and point to new, creative and effective options for brand growth. Later in this section you will see how supercodes naturally crystallize in the strategic and creative process – as in the test case for a cold relief bubble bath below.

4. *Emotional strategies that deliver hard-sell results*: The conventional wisdom is that working with emotions and image is a soft-sell approach. In other words, do not expect any significant, short-term effect in the market. We do not agree. Emotional brands can, in fact, sell better and faster than other brands that focus on a hard benefit. The key is in focusing and modulating the emotional proposition until it is powerful and compelling enough to click with the consumer. An analogy would be the difference between a flashlight and a laser: both project a beam of light, except one of them can be focused to the point that it burns through metal.

5. *Smashing the crystal ball*: Working with growth codes enables you to zero in on what needs to be optimized in your brand strategy and the way to do it. The next time your agency presents a storyboard for a purely emotional brand campaign, you may recognize the elements of the Empathy Principle (cf. Portal 5: Emotions & Love). This in turn enables you to map the proposal against proven success factors, for example:

   - *"The hero's personality is too strong, he should be softer, more vulnerable in order to arouse empathy."*, or
   - *"We need to tighten the dramatic turn, when frustration turns into happiness."*

Growth codes pin down the arguments behind a gut feeling.

6. *Getting more out of market research*: We all know that millions are being spent on market research without having a clear

idea of what to look for. Suppose your mission is to introduce a new soft drink and you hire a market research firm to do the groundwork. How do you define *their* mission? More to the point: what can you do to maximize your benefit from the survey effort? Here, working with growth codes can prove invaluable by laying the blueprint for test design. Your proposed strategy: to make your soft drink a megaphone for your consumers. The idea is to express a character trait your consumers possess or aspire to possess, as in the Character Principle (cf. Portal 4: Identity & Self-expression).

Now, your market research partner can find answers to two meaningful questions:

(i) *What character traits are attributable to the product – based on taste, color, packaging, origin, etc.? (If our soft drink were a person, what would that person be like in the consumer's eyes?)*

(ii) *What are the most important character traits our consumers aspire to and want to have expressed?*

This is how marketing research becomes an invaluable aid in building a solid platform for your new brand strategy. Growth codes help make surveys more focused and cost-efficient by enabling you to define a clear mission. They provide clear questions, which can be answered meaningfully.


## APPLYING GROWTH CODES

The following hypothetical situation illustrates the versatility and flexibility of the blw method.

Our assignment: to market a beer that is positioned with an "origin" theme. The positioning has been consistent over the years. Sales are now declining. How can we use a growth code to leverage our current brand equity? Here are three options.

1. *The Mind-Movie Principle (Portal 1: Benefits & Promises)*: If our beer were brewed in the country – say in the Black Forest – this would enable us to project Black Forest values onto our brand, e.g. "natural, rich, genuine." The idea: A beer like the place it is coming from. This, of course, only works if consumers are attracted to a beer with that "Black Forest taste." Only then does it make sense to script and project a Black Forest mind-movie.

2. *The Emotional Node Principle (Portal 5: Emotions & Love)*: What if the region our beer originates from is primarily known and appreciated for its *cultural heritage*? Here, we tap into the strong emotions of regional allegiance and pride and transfer them onto our beer – "This beer is a part of our culture, our history and our traditions – a part of us." By comparison bigger national beer brands all of a sudden come across as soulless invaders, further elevating the special quality of our brand in the consumer's mind.

3. *The Character Principle (Portal 4: Identity & Self-expression)*: Our beer could also be brewed in a big city – Hamburg, for instance. Here, too, we can build on origins to set the brand on a new track toward growth. One thing many people associate with Hamburg is its world-famous red-light district, the sinful *Reeperbahn*. A rakish, even slightly depraved character can plausibly be quite appealing to consumers who do not want to be perceived as square, uptight or conservative. Here is a beer brand that can express this character trait for them.

And that was just a warm-up. The "origin" theme can no doubt inspire many more possibilities for applying growth codes and developing the strategy that will reverse the downward trend.

In the experience of our own agency, we have had ample opportunity to test growth codes in the most diverse industries – from an automobile club to a cigarette brand, from banks to telecommunications, from a power company to a political party, from cosmetics to pharmaceuticals. The growth codes proved their worth at every juncture and delivered results that exceeded expectations. Just how versatile growth codes can be *within a single industry* is a strength we can demonstrate with three case studies for Siemens mobile phones. Each strategy generated outstanding growth and increased market share for the brand.

## Case Study: Siemens S4 Power Mobile Phone

### *The Background*

German electronics giant Siemens wanted to strengthen and expand its then weak position in Italy's huge and fast-growing telecommunications market. The company's S4 Power product was to be the vanguard.

When we first saw the prototype, we were disappointed: the S4 Power was boring – although practical and functional, its design was bland and brick-like. The only distinctive feature was a then revolutionary 10 hours of talk time before the phone had to be recharged. Market research, however, showed that Italian consumers attached greater importance to long *standby* times, modern design and technical sophistication (read gimmicks). The S4 Power offered none of these. The market situation in Italy was not that much more encouraging:

- Siemens had a 3% share of the market (October 1996) and most consumers had never heard of Siemens.

- The big players on the European market – Nokia, Motorola and Ericsson – had already firmly staked their claims on the Italian territory.

- Siemens was synonymous with powerplants, but not telecommunications, let alone mobile phones.

- While competitors were spending millions on marketing, the budget for the S4 Power totaled just about US$600 000 at the time.

## *The Challenge*

Any which way you looked at it, the only real selling point of the S4 Power was its long talk time of 10 hours. We went back to the market and got confirmation of the fact that most cellphone calls took only a few minutes. Virtually nobody used their mobile phone for long conversations. In other words, 10 hours of talk time was a great solution without a problem. A frustrating situation: we had a unique selling point, but it was irrelevant. Especially so if we looked at the two market leaders:

- Nokia had just introduced a new model whose curvy, ergonomic shape had already made it a favorite among the design-crazed Italians.

- Ericsson had a very compact mobile on the market that fitted into your shirt pocket – very practical for people who always wanted their phone on hand.

By comparison, the S4 Power came across as very bulky and with a sober functionality that was more in line with German intellectual understatement perhaps than with the more lively Italian temperament. The situation was bleak: "We're up against Nokia and Ericsson . . . and all we've got is 10 hours of talk time."

## The Strategy

One thought kept coming up during our internal discussion rounds: mobile phones were still important status symbols. People also bought mobile phones because of the image they projected. A mobile phone definitely characterized you as someone important in today's achiever society. Ironically, it was mostly shoppers, students, homemakers and hipsters who flashed their mobiles out on the sidewalk. In any case, this gave us a good track to run on: our S4 Power could become a megaphone for the consumer. This led us to the Membership Principle (cf. Portal 4: Identity & Self-expression) – we wanted the S4 Power to be the badge of an exclusive social group that consumers were proud to belong to or, more important, *aspired to belong to*:

*The S4 Power is the mobile phone for* true *business professionals. At the same time, users of other mobile phones were exposed as wannabes because they obviously did not know what counts in a mobile phone – what good are fancy design and technical frills if the battery is empty?*

It made sense that business professionals should focus on maximum talktime because they could not afford to have their conversations cut off suddenly as a result of depleted batteries – 10 hours of talktime provided a valuable safety margin.

Yet "business professionals" was still a pretty large and vague universe – it also conjured up frazzled, stressed-out individuals with pale complexions and ulcers. Nobody wants to see themselves as a slave to the job. No, the business professional we had in mind was the sort of achiever who got more accomplished with a few deals than others with years of hard work. He was the bold go-getter who elicited admiration rather than envy.

## *The Bottom Line*

The S4 Power campaign took the Italian market by storm:

- Market share rose from 3% to 11% within three months.
- In the same period distribution increased from 35% to 85%.

## Case Study: Siemens S6 Mobile Phone

## *The Background*

Following the success with the S4 Power, Siemens asked us to stage the introduction of a new mobile phone in Italy – the S6. Visually, the new phone seemed big and flat, but the technology inside was impressive. There were five strong selling points, though each had a weakness:

1. *It was flat*: It was the flattest cellphone in the market – a real step forward and a point you could dramatize. Except it was also long and wide, so it actually came across as bigger and bulkier than its competitors.

2. *It was lightweight*: It weighed only 160 g where others weighed up to 250 g. A strong benefit, but risky to build on because an even lighter competitive phone was being launched in the market.

3. *It was user-friendly*: The S6 had a five-line graphic display that also displayed icons. This made it easy for the user to navigate through menus without having to first learn the manual. A great advantage at first, except it made the phone look like a toy for beginners. The larger overall size, low weight and the competitive price supported the "toy" aspect.

4. *It had good sound quality*: The S6 was the only phone to feature a hi-fi speaker and an advanced electronic noise filter. Excellent product benefits, if it were not for the fact that the

network was the primary factor for transmission (and thus
sound) quality. Here our promise of superior sound quality
could actually backfire through no fault of ours.

5. *It had GSM Phase II capability*: The S6 was the first to give
   users the benefit of so-called GSM Phase II network services
   – caller ID, call forwarding, mailbox, SMS, traffic information,
   etc. A triumph of German engineering that would surely sell.
   Except for the fact that very few people knew what GSM
   stood for and did not know there had been a Phase I to begin
   with – how were we going to start explaining what Phase II was
   about?

These were the facts.

## The Challenge

Successful brand positioning, as we all know, builds on a clear
thought – not five different arguments. We could have selected
the strongest of the five factors and developed a big selling story.
The fact of the matter, though, was that we were not proving that
we were better than everyone else – except for the innovative GSM
Phase II capability. On the other hand, we had five strong benefits and they could not be dismissed so easily.

We could, of course, have taken the easy road and said: "Five
great reasons to buy the Siemens S6." Experience, however,
showed that these unfocused approaches did not deliver solid
growth. Besides, who could remember a whole list of arguments?
The challenge, in other words, was: "How can we distill all these
benefits into one compelling, crystal-clear proposition?"

## The Strategy

The fundamental issue, we realized, was the consumer's perception of the product. Here, the first step was to look behind

Portal 3: Perceptions & Programs. There we hit on the League Principle: "Move your brand into a different, unexpected league in which its strengths can fully unfold."

This inspired us to *establish the S6 as the prototype of a new mobile phone generation*:

- *The Siemens S6 is the vanguard in a "league of its own" – where there are no competitors.*

- *At the same time, we "demote" competitors as obsolete – without saying it in so many words.*

What we had done was to create a *fundamental* shift in the consumer's perception of the mobile phone market. It was no longer about fancy and less fancy models, or more gimmicks vs. fewer gimmicks. Instead of having to compare all the mobile phones and their various features, the consumer had a very simple decision to make: "Am I going to buy the *old* generation or am I going to go with the *new* generation?"

The strategy made the S6 the logical choice. Our claim was corroborated by the fact that our S6 was the *first* to meet GSM Phase II criteria. We did not use this fact as a benefit argument in itself, but "only" as evidence of our claim to be a new generation. Even if the consumer did not need to understand exactly what it meant and we did not need to go into the details, it was nevertheless crucial to *substantiate* our claim.

## *The Bottom Line*

After the S4 campaign had boosted Siemens' market share from 3% to 11%, it was now up to 25%. Both campaigns covered a total period of just eight months. The media budget was US$3.2 million, much less than the industry average. All this goes to show that the key to a brand's success is the strategy behind it.

## Case Study Siemens S10 Mobile Phone

### The Background

As Central European markets were being liberalized, more and more western corporations were establishing subsidiaries in Poland, Rumania, Hungary, the Czech Republic and Turkey. Siemens intended to launch its top-of-the-line S10 mobile phone in the Czech Republic – as the dependable accessory for western executives. The S10 was also the world's first with a color display! It sounded like a sensation, but there were two caveats:

1. The colors were not that brilliant and barely visible in daylight.
2. Market research told us that a color display did not impress businesspeople – it was a gimmick with no obvious useful purpose.

The phone's other technological features – from the noise reduction filter to a memo function – had long become industry standards.

### The Challenge

One thing was clear: color was the only thing going for us. The first step was to add functionality to the color feature. Do not color-coded icons and information make it easier to use? Think about Formula 1 racing where drivers get all their instruction with color flags. On the other hand, the Formula 1 analogy was a stretch. Not likely that this argument would click with business-people in the Czech Republic. We could not extol color brilliance, nor could we call this yet another "new generation". It might have attracted lots of curious people to the phone, but the display would have been a letdown – and a backlash would have surely followed. It would have meant a loss of credibility for Siemens and potential risks for future business. The challenge became more and more of a dilemma: how could we turn the color display into a purchase motive without raising expectations on color brilliance?

## The Strategy

The S10 was an excellent product with the added bonus of a color display. And we knew that an excellent product would sell. It was simply a matter of finding the right growth code. But how does a color display fit in? What is compelling about a color display? As we approached the problem from a growth code perspective, we realized that the question to ask might be, "What is compelling about *not* having a color display?" The S10 was the first mobile phone to make the leap from black and white to color. Regardless of whether a color display was useful or not, it was the next step forward in innovation. Did not that make black and white obsolete? Since a color display put black and white phones behind the times, where did that put consumers? The answer came to us as we explored Portal 2: Norms & Values. . . .

*In business you cannot afford to fall behind and you pride yourself in always being one step ahead. If you are a businessman and still phoning in black and white, you are simply no longer with it.*

In other words, we applied the Pride Principle: "Challenge your consumers and make your brand a means of satisfying it." The result: having a phone with a black and white display was a no-no. The clincher: we were making the color display a decisive purchase motivator – a matter of pride – without raising expectations on color display quality. The issue was color vs. black and white, not color brilliance. Dilemma solved.

## The Bottom Line

During the five months airing time of the campaign, Siemens' market share in the Czech Republic climbed from 2% to 18%.

These three case studies show how different growth codes can be effective for products *within the same industry*. They also show how a growth code can address specific product attributes, market situations and consumer perceptions.

We are now going to run through three test case scenarios to give you an idea of how seemingly impossible marketing challenges can be resolved . . . In each case the brand names have been changed.

## Test Case: A Cold Relief Bubble Bath

### *The Problem*

Nature's Best has been manufacturing natural medicinal products for over a hundred years. One of these is a cold relief bubble bath that eases cold and flu symptoms. How does the product work? Eucalyptus menthol is inhaled via the nose and simultaneously transported into the bloodstream via the skin.

The market for cold relief bubble baths is declining rapidly, however, slipping 15% to 20% every year. This also has a significant effect on Nature's Best's sales. Fewer and fewer consumers believe that cold relief bubble baths actually help. They cannot picture how the medication actually helps relieve the symptoms. A further problem resides in the fact that people do not think of taking a cold relief bubble bath when they have a cold, but instead rely on a nasal spray, cough syrup or other medication. Cold relief bubble baths are not top-of-mind. And they do not necessarily catch the consumer's attention in the supermarket or the drugstore because they are displayed among other bubble baths, oil baths, care baths, relaxing baths, revitalizing baths, etc. No wonder the consumer overlooks them.

The situation is serious. Nature's Best also has to contend with two major competitors. The market leader is MediCure, followed by Aquasan. Nature's Best is a distant third. All three have the same active ingredient; namely, eucalyptus menthol. Unfortunately, Nature's Best contains less of the active ingredient than its two competitors. Clearly not an avenue for challenging the competition. Compounding the problem, MediCure is very vocal in claiming to be the number one in the market and has the consumer's trust. After all, if you're the number one, your product has to be better than the competition. Yet Aquasan also has a strong suit: the brand is well-established with a long-standing tradition in medicated bubble bath therapy – a competence Nature's Best cannot match either.

The two competitors are also setting high standards in their marketing communications. The TV commercials show glass bathtubs, lots of skin, beautiful women, soft lighting and soothing classical music.

To recap: the market is shrinking and the only two competitors seem unbeatable in every respect. Now it is your turn. Find a brand positioning that will make Nature's Best grow and beat the competition. There is a solution: look for the growth code that fits.

## Strategic Recommendation

Conventional wisdom tells us that people come down with a cold or the flu on average twice a year. Germany with its 80 million or so inhabitants would theoretically account for 160 million purchase occasions. How then could our small market for cold relief bubble baths be declining? We find a surprising explanation when we look at our consumer's perception. Into which mental drawer do consumers put cold relief bubble baths? In the one that is labeled "Bubble Baths" or in the one that says "Cold Medication"? It turns out that most people place Nature's Best's product in the former. And for good reasons:

- In the supermarket, all cold relief bubble baths are on the same shelf as regular bubble baths – not in the flu and cold medication section.

- The two main competitors position themselves primarily as bubble baths; namely, with glass bathtubs, naked women, glamorous settings in their brand communication.

This virtually forces consumers to see cold relief bubble baths as just a different kind of bubble bath – and not as the cold relief therapy it is. This has three major consequences:

1. Anybody who has a cold first looks in his or her "Cold Medication" mental drawer for relief. Since Nature's Best is not even in the drawer to begin with, it has no chance. The same thing happens in the supermarket: consumers looking around in the cold medication section will not spot Nature's Best because it is in a completely different aisle.

2. Even the few that come across Nature's Best in the bubble bath section are confused because a bubble bath is primarily associated with a cosmetic rather than a therapeutic purpose. The more a cold relief bubble bath is positioned as a "Bubble Bath" (as MediCure and Aquasan), the less consumers will buy into its medicinal properties.

3. A bubble bath also comes with a specific "mental user manual" that is not at all in line with Nature's Best's therapy program:

   - People take a bubble bath once a week or even less frequently, while Nature's Best delivers better therapeutic results if used once a day during a seven-day period (as long as the symptoms persist).

   - Bubble baths are preferred by female consumers (2 to 1) while Nature's Best is a cold relief therapy for both genders.

- Bubble baths are usually taken by older consumers, whereas Nature's Best can and should be used at all ages as a cold or flu therapy.

These are all very compelling reasons for taking Nature's Best out of the "Bubble Bath" mental drawer! We are moving closer and closer to the Migration Principle: " Migrate into a different, unexpected mental drawer where your brand can better unfold." In our specific case this means:

*We take Nature's Best out of the mental drawer marked "Bubble Baths" and place it without equivocation into the mental drawer of "Cold Medication." Nature's Best is now in a much larger market than before. It is now also perceived as an additional therapy for cold and flu symptoms.*

At the same time, and this is crucial, the sales and distribution team is instructed to have Nature's Best placed in the "Cold Medication" section at supermarkets, drugstores and pharmacies.

We have now successfully repositioned the brand and created a compelling purchase motive by redefining the consumer's perception of the product. The question now is what can we do to firmly establish our competence as a cold relief therapy and differentiate us from our new competitors? What can we do to really click with the consumer?

As research has shown, consumers have no clear idea how the cold relief bubble bath transfers its therapeutic effects to the body. The factual explanation is simple: the hot bathtub water dilates the pores, which allows the active ingredients to get in the bloodstream. Put this way, it is not only scientific, but perhaps even disquieting. This is a good track to run on, however, for our second strategic thrust. It points to the *magic* in *Nature's Best*.

From our earliest childhood we know how effective inhalation is in fighting a cold – we breathe in the menthol and eucalyptus and it frees our sinuses, giving us immediate relief. We also know that skin breathes. Here is the magic: the idea of an *inhalation therapy* for the skin. Although this does not fit in with our conventional understanding of processes at first, it does make for an *intriguing implausibility* that captures the imagination. And it fits with Nature's Best's product effect – it is the magic action that explains how Nature's Best works. By establishing Nature's Best as "an inhalation therapy for the whole body" we promise much more than the simple factual evidence. We give the customer a new experience.

To recap: we have taken Nature's Best out of the small and limited-growth market of bubble baths and positioned it in the much larger market for cold relief medication (Migration Principle). Within the market of cold medication, Nature's Best is now invested with a magical property: it is the inhalation therapy for the whole body (Magic Principle). Here, we combined two already powerful growth codes into an even more compelling supercode.

Is this the only strategy for success? Why should it be? You may perhaps arrive at a completely different, equally effective solution. One way to ensure that your strategy will work and click with the consumer is to make sure it makes sense. It has to pass the common sense test. Run the idea by your friends and colleagues and see if they follow the logic of your argumentation as clearly and easily as you did. If you pass that test, the chances are good that your positioning will also work in the market.

## Test Case: A Radio Station

### *The Problem*

Ultrawave is a radio station that has been broadcasting for 10 years and is the region's market leader. But now there is a new kid on the block, and he wants your lunch.

Let us first find out more about Ultrawave. One thing you immediately notice is how lively Ultrawave's programming is:

- The announcers are witty, spontaneous and intelligent. They are engaging characters and they often chat with listeners – at the expense of music programming.

- Listeners are actively invited to participate: they can call in with their take on the day's events and issues. There is even a "Blind Date Line" for lonely hearts.

- Ultrawave offers useful services, e.g. regular announcements of speed trap locations.

- The programming is always live on air – they never play tapes, even during the night.

- New tracks are played before they become mainstream hits. Ultrawave is not afraid of trying out something new and risk missing the audience's taste.

- Big promotional events are also a regular feature. One example is a treasure hunt that has listeners scampering around the countryside looking for a small fortune buried somewhere – but they have to listen in regularly or they will miss important clues.

The Ultrawave concept has been very successful, especially with the 20–39 age group. Things take a dramatic turn, however, when a new station, part of a nationwide franchise, starts broadcasting in the same region: Radiostar. It is less a radio station than a smooth and highly efficient marketing machine. Every week, newspaper articles tell how Radiostar is taking over the whole country, one region at a time. Behind the station we have an army of marketing professionals who have perfected the art of tailoring their product to the masses.

- Virtually non-stop top hits of the "easy listening" kind. Almost no talk or journalism. Listeners like it and it saves costs.

- The few announcers they have are seasoned professionals who do not go out on a limb – listeners are never provoked, there is never a spontaneous or off-hand remark. Announcers basically only have the function of reading off news and traffic information. Nighttime programming is from the reel.

- New songs are aired only after they are well on the charts. Every song fits in with mainstream listening tastes. The strategy is: "Don't take chances!"
- Their idea of variety is to play Top 10 hits from the past decade.
- Games, promotions and other entertaining programming are kept to a minimum.

Radiostar, however, is fast becoming a winner in Ultrawave's territory, especially in the large 30–50 age group. A typical survey comment: "I used to listen a lot to Ultrawave, but now it's just too loud and too wild. That's why I switched over to Radiostar." The new kid on the block is seriously eroding Ultrawave's position.

The big problem, it seems, is that listeners actually prefer Radiostar's programming. Each one of them at some point made the conscious decision that Ultrawave is "just not for me anymore." A personal value judgment like that is hard to refute. More variety, more entertainment and better quality do not cut it anymore. Should Ultrawave review the strategy that had been so successful until now? Out of the question: that would be tantamount to rolling over – and giving up any chance of regaining the upper hand.

Sound impossible? Give it a try and develop a strategy for Ultrawave that not only secures its share of the market, but also increases it against Radiostar. What would you do?

### Strategic Recommendation 1

The first step is to simplify the problem. What are the issues? What sets the two stations apart? How can we draw a clear line between them? By mapping the two against each other, we reach one clear polarization: Ultrawave is young – and Radiostar is old. Let us verify: what makes Ultrawave so young?

- A younger audience
- Witty, zesty and laid-back announcers
- Spontaneous, live programming
- Lots of games and promotions

And what makes Radiostar old?

- An older audience
- Predictable, smooth, standard programming
- Safe hits (no brand new tracks)

What we have done is to establish a platform for a strategy. Here we hit on a very promising thought: "Young vs. Old." This contrast not only characterizes the two stations against each other, but also profiles the two audiences. As in "Tell me what station you listen to and I'll tell you who you are" the choice of radio station says something about its listeners and that leads us to Portal 4: Identity & Self-expression in the consumer's mind – and from there to the Character Principle.

**The idea:** *Tuning in to Ultrawave says you are "young in spirit," whereas listening to Radiostar points you out as being "old in spirit." We are not talking biological age: an 80-year-old can still* **be** *pretty young in spirit, and a 20-year-old the worst sort of reactionary.*

The strategy has the effect of splitting the population into two camps: the "young" ones who listen to Ultrawave and the "old" ones who listen to Radiostar. If you want to be perceived as youthful, hip and with it, then tuning in to Radiostar sends the wrong message. This also has the effect of turning the moment a listener wants to switch from Ultrawave to Radiostar into a taboo.

The idea here: "You know you're getting old when you switch from Ultrawave to Radiostar." Switching radio stations no longer has anything to do with choosing what you like better! Instead, it becomes a threshold moment like your fiftieth birthday that tells you you are getting old!

The idea of "young in spirit" opens all sorts of possibilities for implementing the strategy. The core idea is a big promotion event under the motto, "The Ultrawave Age Check: How old are you *really*?" A promotion team roams the region's pubs, bars and cafés and runs patrons through a brief, provocative psychological test to determine their "true" age. Imagine the hooting when a 25-year-old college student answers a few questions and it turns out his mental age is 68 – or a 70-year-old lady who turns out to be sweet sixteen. At all times, it is clear that "young" people listen to Ultrawave while "older" people listen to Radiostar.

Pass the Age Check test and if your mental age is under 30, you are issued an Ultrawave Pass with your "real age" on it that also gives you a discount to "youth" cultural events in the region – concerts, openings, avant-garde theater, etc.

The promotion is easy to capitalize on on-air as well. Example: a young female listener calls up complaining about her 23-year-old boyfriend who goes to bed with his socks on – "Could you find out his real age for me?" Our Ultrawave announcers leap at the opportunity and call the unsuspecting fellow at work the next day – all this is on the air – and run him through the Age Check to the amusement of his girlfriend, colleagues and all the other listeners. Within a few months, getting exposed as "old in spirit" becomes embarrassing. And liking Radiostar becomes less and less acceptable. Ultrawave is number one again!

### Strategic Recommendation 2

You could draw another kind of line between Ultrawave and Radiostar, opening a different strategic option and a new growth code. It builds on an "us vs. them" platform: Ultrawave is the *home* station, Radiostar is the *intruder*.

- Ultrawave is, after all, The Original that has become part of the cultural landscape over the past ten years.
- The programming is regional, by announcers who grew up in the region.
- Ultrawave is proud of its roots and attached to the region. Ultrawave gets involved, is interested in what the people in the region do, and tells their stories.

Just as clear is Radiostar's position as the stranger:

- The new radio station is an intruder.
- Instead of getting involved with the people from the region, Radiostar basically regurgitates the same standard fare it has got planned for the whole nation.
- There is no regional touch, just a smooth marketing machine at work.

This strategic platform opens Portal 5: Emotions & Love to the Emotional Node principle. In our case, this means:

*We tap into the strong feelings of regional pride within the population and fuse them with Ultrawave. Listeners like the station because they love it and because they love their region. At the same time, this has the effect of further stigmatizing Radiostar as the intruder who believes he can get away with a one-size-fits-all programming strategy designed for the whole country.*

The net result is that of erecting an emotional barrier against Radiostar with the objective that people demonstratively boycott the intruding radio station. Even if the programming were to be objectively better, the fact that the intruder is the one broadcasting makes it suspect.

How do we implement the strategy? Our guiding thought here: it is about feelings of love. The more I love something, the more sensitive I am to anybody or anything that might threaten it. Imagine if someone were to offer the city of Paris a huge sum of money for the Eiffel Tower – just for the metal. You can picture the outcry! It also shows how intense the feelings for the Eiffel Tower can be when called upon.

This latent emotion is something we can tap into. How? Imagine a stealthy overnight operation in which signs are put throughout the entire region: "Down with Ultrawave! We want national radio!" What an affront to the people! They are going to shut down Ultrawave? Closing down a regional treasure just so an anonymous broadcaster can send out nationwide standard programming? It is the kind of provocation that can shake people awake and win them over to Ultrawave. Not only that: anybody listening to Radiostar could very well be suspected of high treason . . .

Ultrawave might take it a step further and expose Radiostar's power-hungry expansion plans. News of the impending scheme to overrun the region and the whole country with standard easy listening is tantamount to a brainwashing campaign. This would galvanize the population into building a *Résistance* against the evil invader.

We have now presented two growth codes that will effectively put Ultrawave back on top. Interestingly enough, neither approach focuses on the programming. Instead, it clicks with the consumer on an emotional level. And it is just as hard-selling.

## Test Case: A Lip Balm

### *The Problem*

Everybody knows what it is like: in cold dry weather or in the burning sun your lips start to feel dry and sensitive. There has been a product on the market for over a hundred years to soothe your lips and protect them: Softlip is a lip balm that contains only a natural fat – no other active agent. But it works. So well in fact that Softlip has become synonymous with lip balm (just like Pampers with diapers and Kleenex with facial tissues).

But times are changing: for two years now Liposan has been aggressively building up market share. In addition to a natural fat, Liposan contains an *active* medicinal ingredient to accelerate the healing process. The brand is positioned as the more modern, more effective alternative to our "old-fashioned" traditional product. The message is driven home clearly to consumers with humorous and aggressive TV commercials. One of them, for instance, shows us a young, hip female model with brightly colored hair and lips that are so dry that lint sticks on them when she pulls a sweater over her head. Good thing she has a Liposan stick to make her lips soft and smooth again! Liposan strikes a chord with consumers and within just a few months the new brand owns 15% of the market. Is there any reason people should still buy Softlip? After all, everybody knows that it only contains a natural fat.

Suppose you were responsible for marketing Softlip – what would be your strategy to fight Liposan? How would you proceed to stop Liposan's inexorable advance? How would you put your foot down? One thing, though: we are not going to change the formula or alter the product in any way – Softlip will remain a lip balm that contains only a pure, natural fat. So, what are you going to do?

## Strategic Recommendation

One thing is absolutely clear: there is no way we can prove we are *better* than Liposan. But if we cannot be better, we certainly can be *different*. The strategic discussions on this point finally lead us to a viable strategy behind Portal 3: Perceptions

& Programs; namely, the Territory Principle (to reposition competitors).

What we are going to do is relegate Liposan into the smallest possible territory: *"medication for lip ailments"*. This highly specialized niche makes up only 5% of the market. Now we claim the remaining majority of the market for Softlip: *"general everyday lip care"*. This covers about 95% of the market. Softlip can easily live with the fact that the few people who might grudgingly acknowledge that they have a *lip problem* will gravitate to Liposan. Using Liposan now implies that the consumer is suffering from a chronic lip problem.

As we can see, applying this variant of the Territory Principle enables us to mark a territory within the market for lip care products that actually represents the larger portion of that market. At the same time, our new – initially fierce – competitor is now relegated into a much smaller niche. What is remarkable is that we do not even have to acknowledge or attack Liposan. On the contrary, the new competitor's own positioning backfires because it comes across as *medication* which only makes the product relevant to the consumer with a lip ailment – and might even imply that frequent, indiscriminate use is probably not a good idea.

## SUMMARY

We have run through six different scenarios for working with growth codes: three describe strategies that have been actually developed and implemented by the authors, and three test cases. What transpires in all clarity is this:

1. Growth codes are a *practical* tool for developing winning strategies to increase sales and market share, regardless of the product or service. Regardless of whether it is for mobile phones, a cold relief bubble bath, radio station or a lip balm.

2. Working with growth codes enables you to develop strategies that address your marketing problem more effectively and directly than ever before. Do not say, "My problem is too specific or too complex for growth codes." That would be the same as if a repairman said, "This problem is too specific or complex to be solved by using *tools*!" The truth is that the more complex the task, the greater the chances of resolving it with a systematic approach and the right tools, i.e. growth codes.

3. Growth codes are not magic formulas that purport to replace the strategic and creative process. Their role is to stimulate thought processes, and open new possibilities by enabling you to think outside the box.

4. Growth codes are about making brand growth something you can plan and achieve systematically. They do not give you a better crystal ball. They are a way of maximizing your brand investment and getting the best odds on your side.

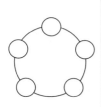

# Taking Growth Codes Into the Internet Age

To say that our idea to tap the vast experience of the world's most successful brands did not raise any eyebrows when we first began propounding the concept would not even be close to the truth. Some old hands in the brand business were even vehemently opposed to the idea. What could there possibly be left to learn about brands that everybody did not already know? Also, the thought of *methodically* arriving at an effective positioning for a specific product or service in a specific market for a specific group of consumers flew in the face of conventional wisdom. To conservative minds, *method* sounded too much like "restrictive thinking" and "standard solutions."

The speed of change, however, is unforgiving and marketing simply cannot afford to inch along on the slow lane of the information superhighway. The future is *knowledge management* – the idea of centrally collecting the aggregate knowledge of worldwide marketing in a gigantic database and keeping decision-makers from reinventing the wheel. Imagine, being able to extract exactly those ideas, strategies and information which are relevant to solving the marketing problem you face today.

## THE MARKETING PORTAL IN THE INTERNET

As more and more business processes are being shifted to the Internet, brand professionals will be working through Marketing Portals, to access the complete spectrum of marketing services. It is about a workable platform for individualized marketing as opposed to mass marketing. The Marketing Portal covers the following areas:

1. Positioning consulting
2. Marketing planning
3. Direct marketing
4. Sales support and promotion
5. Public relations
6. Market research
7. Media planning and consulting

and more.

Marketing services are delivered via a graphical user interface that is linked to a central database of thousands of marketing case studies. Customers can also purchase traditional agency development and production services: from a simple sales flier to a full-blown TV campaign. Behind the Marketing Portal, everything is just a mouse click away.

The services provided by the Marketing Portal are comprehensive. Here is a brief overview of what the system can do.

1. *Positioning consulting*: The customer can access a dialogue-oriented expert system on-screen that flows much the same

way as conversation with a real person. "What is the name of your brand?" – "Who are your consumers?" – "What is your marketing objective?", and so on. The computer uses each answer to formulate the next question and zero in on the customer's marketing problem. After a maximum of 20 questions, the system accesses a database and suggests a growth code to solve the problem. Case studies are supplied to corroborate the selection of the growth code – much the same way as in this book.

2. *Marketing planning*: This electronic consultant devises a marketing plan that can be tailored to a specific

   - Product type
   - Marketing goal,
   - Target group
   - Budget
   - Region and
   - Timeframe

   The system presents a straightforward marketing plan, tailored to your requirements. This graphical representation not only contains all relevant milestones, but also optimizes synergies and offers interactive edititing capabilities. WAP-technology, for instance, will soon enable decision-makers to view and work with the marketing plan any time anywhere, from some future iteration of what we still call "mobile phone."

3. *Direct marketing*: The Marketing Portal offers a portfolio of proven direct response packages, individually selectable by mouse click. Once the customer has chosen a specific package, the order is processed immediately and passed on to a copywriter and completed at a set rate within a few days – if requested, in several languages as well. The customer can access the addresses of his consumers on-screen and print

labels out within seconds: the Marketing Portal is connected with international list brokers and, on the basis of the information provided, the system will even suggest *new*, potentially profitable target groups that may not have been considered by the customer.

4. *Sales support and promotion*: As we know, many consumers make their purchase decisions at the Point of Sale (POS). The electronic consultant knows that, too, and will produce new ideas and suggestions for generating purchase impulses via promotions and sales support measures. The plan is to enable customers to develop their own promotions on-line by tapping the experiences of numerous successful promotions implemented in the past.

5. *Public relations*: An electronic assistant helps the user put together press releases and information kits. Here, he can choose from a number of stored formats for the most diverse applications as well as receive e-mail addresses and contact numbers to the most important trade magazines. Within 20 minutes it is possible to mail up to 150 publishers and service them with breaking news.

6. *Market research*: The Marketing Portal will take the initiative of informing clients of new industry surveys and publications that can be conveniently ordered via mouse click. Intelligent search robots will scour the Internet for answers to full text questions, not just key words, and deliver findings conveniently sorted.

7. *Media planning and consulting*: The Marketing Portal is connected with professional media agencies that will develop a comprehensive media plan according to the customer's marketing objective and budget requirements – including print advertising, TV commercials, newspapers, magazines, billboards and cinema. Media commissions – in Germany an

average of 15% – directly flow back to the customer via the Marketing Portal.

And who will log on?

1. *Medium-size businesses*: They want professional marketing know-how at competitive rates. The Marketing Portal is their one-stop shop for marketing and communication services.

2. *Consumer goods manufacturers/corporations*: They use the Marketing Portal as a resource in their own intranet. Here, *internal* data warehousing is combined with the Marketing Portal's *external* services, significantly speeding up project turnaround times.

3. *Service companies*: These include financial services, insurance companies and trade fairs. Here, the Marketing Portal enables them to extend their portfolio of services to their own customers. It is a tool for adding value as well as acquiring new customers.

4. *Institutions, organizations, government administrations*: Ministries and economic development agencies already today are implementing plans to expand existing marketing platforms to promote growth in a region and even an entire state.

The Marketing Portal will contain advanced one-to-one technology to provide *individualized* service – specific to the customer's industry, company, corporate design and other topics. As a result, the system gets to know its customers better and better over time. The Marketing Portal can then be even more proactive and provide information on an ongoing basis. Example: a customer in the textile industry will automatically be informed of a fashion show, complete with dates and deadlines – and an offer to arrange and coordinate the customer's presence at the fair at a fixed rate. Naturally, all data will be protected using the most sophisticated cryptographic keys and extensive firewalls.

Far from being a phantasy, the first steps toward making this marketing dream become reality, have already been taken – at www.white-lion.com. Behind this marketing portal, you will find the b|w-method and the growth codes are already delivering solutions as an expert system. Simply click on the *Growth Code Finder* under *Positioning Consulting*.

## THE B|W METHOD AS AN EXPERT SYSTEM

Let us now explore one service in greater detail; namely, the Growth Code Finder. For the purposes of illustrating the application's potential we have deliberately chosen a simplified case. Let us suppose your marketing mission is to market a color laundry detergent called Clear. A color laundry detergent is formulated to protect colors and may even enhance brilliance. Though Clear was the inventor of color laundry detergents, it is now being pushed against the wall by a main competitor Shiny. Shiny has a brand new formula that delivers more brilliant colors, more so than Clear. Consumers are impressed and Shiny skyrockets to 70% of the market while Clear is gradually losing ground. Do you believe Clear can still be saved? If so, with which positioning? Think about it for a few minutes before we observe how the Growth Code Finder attacks the problem . . .

We begin by entering the product name as well as salient marketing information and our Electronic Positioning Consultant involves us in the following dialogue. . . .

---

*Screenshot 1:*

Which industry, which market or which category does Clear belong in? Please be as precise as you can in your answer, using one single term: _____

---

That was easy. Clear is, as we know, a color laundry detergent. We input this information into the space reserved, press "enter" and the next question comes up. . . .

---

*Screenshot 2:*

What is the *current* brand strategy (i.e. positioning) for Clear? In other words: Why should consumers *currently* prefer Clear to competing products?

_____

---

Here, the system wants to know what the status quo is so that we can compare it with a *new* strategy later on. What do we enter here? At this time, there seems to be only one single sales argument; namely: "Clear is the inventor of the color laundry detergent. Consumers should prefer Clear because of its superior experience and competence." We know that this strategy is a bit weak, but so far we have not come up with anything better. On we go. . . .

---

*Screenshot 3:*

Who are the main competitors Clear would like to gain market share from?
1. In the "home" market (i.e. *color laundry detergent*)
2. Special case: a specific or a few specific main competitors; namely _____
3. Special case: a related or completely different market; namely _____

We click on the *second* option and enter Shiny as our main competitor: Shiny now has 70% of the market – and that is where we see our potential for growth. Let us see what the Electronic Positioning Consultant does with this information. . . .

---

*Screenshot 4:*

What is the competitor's (Shiny) biggest strength?

1. An especially strong quality?
2. An especially strong emotional image?

---

Obviously we are going to select the first option because Shiny stands for quality; namely, *brilliant colors.* The second option would probably be more appropriate for a brand like cigarettes that builds on emotional values. Our Electronic Positioning Consultant digs deeper. . . .

---

*Screenshot 5:*

Does your main competitor (Shiny) have an apparent weakness that consumers might not be aware of?
1. Yes
2. No

---

Unfortunately not, so we click on the second button. We are not going to get off the hook that easily: *Shiny* has no obvious weakness. How then are we going to challenge the brand? The Electronic Positioning Consultant is not done yet . . .

---

*Screenshot 6:*

If you compare your main competitor (Shiny) with Clear, what are the competitor's main strengths? Please describe with one word: _____

Please describe in greater detail (max. 5 sentences):

_____

---

There is no way around it: Shiny's biggest strength is *brilliance*. The detailed descriptive: "Shiny has a new revolutionary formula that makes colors more brilliant than Clear."

At this stage, the Electronic Positioning Consultant ends the dialogue and processes its memory bank for a solution based on a growth code and the b|w method. The following text appears on-screen, ready to be printed out:

---

**Positioning Strategy for Clear Laundry Detergent**

*Situation:*

The market is evolving constantly. Shorter innovation cycles and time-to-market times combined with more and more aggressive competition have made it necessary to review Clear's current positioning, i.e.

*Clear is the inventor of the color laundry detergent. Consumers should prefer Clear because of its superior experience and competence.*

The new strategy must be targeted at new growth. What are the reasons we can give consumers to consciously choose Clear and not a competing product, i.e. Shiny?

**Recommended Growth Code:
The Reinterpretation Principle**

*"Clear should reinterpret a strength of your key competitor Shiny ('brilliant colors') into a negative meaning, significance or value. Contrast your own brand as a positive to that negative."*

And what strength are we talking about here?
Shiny has a new revolutionary formula, which results in more brilliant colors.

(graphic button) Success factors

(graphic button) Sample Case Study

Okay, here we have our growth code: the Reinterpretation Principle. Our mission, now, is to reinterpret brilliance as a weakness.... But how? The answer is close at hand: brilliant colors can only be achieved by adding new chemicals (!) to the detergent. This is where we can nail Shiny. The consumer must learn that *Shiny stands for* chemically *brilliant colors.*

And the best part is that Shiny actually supports our strategy every time it praises its *revolutionary new formula.* This in fact implies a strong reliance on chemicals – and effectively makes Shiny's own brand strategy backfire.

So much for the primary thrust of the strategy. As a *key* success factor of this particular growth code, the Growth Code Finder recommends clearly *demarcating* Clear from Shiny. This is now also much easier and logical: *Clear stands for* naturally *brilliant colors.* All it means is that Clear uses *fewer* chemicals than Shiny. We can now proceed with implementing the strategy and our Electronic Positioning Consultant tells us exactly what other general success factors are relevant to the new strategy . . .

This concludes the test session with our Growth Code Finder. Again, we chose a simple marketing problem to illustrate the basic mechanics. How did the system perform? What do you believe the consumer will prefer to buy: Shiny and its chemically brilliant colors, or Clear with its slightly less brilliant but more natural colors? Exactly! Millions of homemakers do not want more chemicals than necessary in their lives – neither for themselves, nor for their family. In all probability Clear is now the logical choice again.

Remember how insoluble Clear's market problem seemed at the beginning? Yet together with the Growth Code Finder we arrived at a solution relatively quickly. You could surely have developed an effective solution without any electronic help, but it would probably have taken a lot longer. You might also have had to hire external professionals and paid a substantial sum for their competence.

Please bear in mind that we have uncovered only a microscopic facet of the potential of our Growth Code Finder. We could have explored a number of different solutions for the same problem.

We are standing at the threshold of an important development process. We intend to examine hundreds of winning brands every year, enhance our database with their success factors and keep refining our Growth Code Finder. One could compare it to the evolution of chess computers. They, too, were fed with the experience and rules of the world's best chess matches in history – until Deep Blue finally defeated Grand Master Kasparov. The computer and its strategic method was thus able to defeat the genius of Kasparov. Why should a similar development not be possible in marketing as well?

There's more to find out behind the marketing portal* . . .

**www.white-lion.com**

*Available in English from Spring 2000

# BIBLIOGRAPHY

## THE ROAD TO A NEW METHOD

Aaker, D.A. (1982) Positioning Your Brand, *Business Horizons*, **25** (May/June).

Aaker, D.A. (1992) *Management des Markenwerts*, Frankfurt am Main.

Abraham, M. and Lodish, L. (1989) *Advertising Works: A Study of Advertising Effectiveness and the Resulting Strategies and Tactical Implications.* Chicago, IL: Information Resources.

Arndt, J. (ed.) (1968) *Insights into Consumer Behavior*, Boston.

Bandura, A. (1969) *Principles of Behavior Modification.* New York.

Barthes, R. (1964) *Mythologies.* Paris, 1957. *Mythen des Alltags.* Frankfurt am Main.

Behrens, G. (1991) *Konsumentenverhalten*, 2nd Edition. Heidelberg.

Berelson, B. and Steiner, G.A. (1972) *Menschliches Verhalten, Grundlegende Ergebnisse empirischer Forschung. Bd. II: Soziale Aspekte*, Weinheim.

Berelson, B. and Steiner, G.A. (1974) *Menschliches Verhalten, Grundlegende Ergebnisse empirischer Forschung, Vol. I: Forschungsmethoden/Individuelle Aspekte*, 3rd Edition (1974); *Vol. 2: Soziale Aspekte*, 1st Edition (1972). Weinheim.

Bettmann, J.R. (1979) *An Information Processing Theory of Consumer Choice.* Reading, MA: Addison-Wesley.

Biel, A.L. (1993) Converting Image Into Equity, in: D.A. Aaker and A.L. Biel (eds.), *Brand Equity & Advertising.* Hillsdale, NJ: Lawrence Erlbaum Associates.

Brehm, S.S. and Kassin, S.M. (1990) *Social Psychology.* Boston u.a.

Chattopadhyay, A. and Basu, K. (1990) Humor in Advertising: The Moderating Role of Prior Brand Evaluation, *Journal of Marketing Research*, **27** (4), 466–476.

Chattopadhyay, A. and Alba, J.W. (1988) The Situational Importance of Recall and Inference in Consumer Decision Making, *Journal of Consumer Research*, 15 (June).

Cheskin, L. (1957) *How to Predict What People Buy.* New York.

Clark, L.H. (ed.) (1958) *Consumer Behavior. Research in Consumer Reactions.* New York.

Crimmins, J.C. (1992) Better Measurement and Management of Brand Equity, *Fourth Annual ARF Advertising and Promotion Workshop*, February 12–13.

Dichter, E. (1961) *The Strategy of Desire.* New York.

Dichter, E. (1964) *Handbook of Consumer Motivations – The Psychology of the World of Objects.* New York.

Diehl, J.M. (1977) Motivationsforschung im Bereich des Konsumentenverhaltens; in: Todt (ed.), *Motivation*, pp. 237–289.

Dieterich, M. (1986) *Konsument und Gewohnheit.* Heidelberg.

Dieterle, G.S. (1992) *Verhaltenswirksame Bildmotive in der Werbung.* Heidelberg.

Domizlaff, H. (1992) *Die Gewinnung des öffentlichen Vertrauens.* Hamburg.

Dröge, F., Weißenborn, R. and Haft, H. (1973) *Wirkungen der Massenkommunikation, Münster 1969.* Frankfurt am Main.

Engel, J.F., Blackwell, R.D. and Kollat, D.T. (1978) *Consumer Behavior*, 3rd Edition. Hillsdale.

Farquhar, P.H., Han, J.Y., Herr, P.M. and Ijiri, Y. (1992) Strategies for Leveraging Master Brands, *Marketing Research*, September, pp. 32–43.

Fishbein, M. and Ajzen, I. (1975) *Belief, Attitude, Intention and Behavior: An Introduction to Theory and Research*. Reading, MA: Addison-Wesley.

Fishbein, M. and Ajzen, I. (1974) Attitudes Towards Objects as Predictions of Single and Multiple Behavioral Criteria, in *Psychological Review*, January.

GWA (Hg.) (1992) *Effizienz in der Werbung 1993*. Frankfurt.

GWA (Hg.) (1994) *So wirk Werbung in Deutschland*. Frankfurt.

GWA (Hg.) (1994) *Wie man den Erfolg von Werbung mißt*. Frankfurt.

GWA (Hg.) (1996) *Effizienz in der Werbung 1996*. Frankfurt.

GWA (Hg.) (1997) *So wirkt Werbung im Marketing Mix. Die neue Effektivität der Werbung*. Empirische Studie von GWA/GfK. Frankfurt am Main.

Heckhausen, H. (1980) *Motivation und Handeln*. Berlin.

Heckhausen, H. (1989) *Motivation und Handeln*. 2nd Edition. Berlin u.a.

Heller, E. (1996) *Wie Werbung wirkt: Theorien und Tatsachen*. Frankfurt am Main.

Herber, H.-J. (1976) *Motivationspsychologie*. Stuttgart.

Herrmann, A. (1992) *Produktwahlverhalten*. Stuttgart.

Herzig, O.A. (1991) *Markenbilder/Markenwelten – Neue Wege in der Imageforschung*. Wien.

Holzschuher, L. von (1956) *Psychologische Grundlagen der Werbung*. Essen.

Hovland, C.I. *et al.* (1953) *Communication and Persuasion*. New Haven: Yale University Press.

Hoyer, W.D. and Brown, S.P. (1990) Effects of Brand Awareness on Choice for a Common, Repeat-Purchase Product, *Journal of Consumer Research*, 17, 141–148.

Hull, C.L. (1943) *Principles of Behavior*. New York.

Interbrand Group (1992) *World's Greatest Brands. An International Review*. New York: John Wiley & Sons.

Janik, A., Rieke, R. and Toulmin, S. (1979) *An Introduction to Reasoning*, 2nd Edition. New York/London.

Jones, J.P., Brandes, B. and Haller, P. (1995) *How to Measure Sales Success by Media Advertising*. Frankfurt am Main.

Jones, J.P., Brandes, B. and Haller, P. (1995) *So wirkt Werbung in Deutschland. When Ads Work. The German Version.* Frankfurt am Main.

Kanfer, F.H. and Goldstein, A.P. (1977) *Möglichkeiten der Verhaltensänderung.* München, Wien, Baltimore: Urban & Schwarzenberg.

Kaufmann, K. (1975) Kognitiv-hedonistische Theorie menschlichen Verhaltens. Versuch einer Integration verhaltens-theoretischer Ansätze. Dissertation, Mannheim.

Kotler, P.L. (1997) *Marketing Management*, 9th Edition. Upper Saddle River, NJ: Prentice-Hall.

Kroeber-Riel, W. and Meyer-Hentschel, G. (1982) *Werbung – Steuerung des Konsumentenverhaltens.* Würzburg.

Kroeber-Riel, W. (1992) *Konsumentenverhalten*, 5. Aufl. München.

Kroeber-Riel, W. (1993) *Bildkommunikation. Imagerystrategien für die Werbung.* München.

Kroeber-Riel, W. (1993) *Strategie und Technik der Werbung*, 4th Edition. Stuttgart u.a.

Kroeber-Riel, W. (1993) *Strategie und Technik der Werbung – verhaltenswissenschaftliche Ansätze*, 4th Edition. Stuttgart u.a.

Kroeber-Riel, W. (1996) *Konsumentenverhalten.* Saarbrücken.

Krugman, H.E. (1975) What Makes Advertising Effective? *Harvard Business Review*, **53** (March/April), 96–103.

Lattin, J.M. and Bucklin, R.E. (1989) Reference Effects of Price and Promotion on Brand Choice Behavior, *Journal of Marketing Research*, **26** (3), 299–310.

Lebensmittel-Praxis (1997) *Extra 3/97.* Frankfurt.

Light, L. (1994) Bringing Research to the Brand Equity Process, *ARF Brand Equity Workshop*, February 15–16.

Lindgren, H.C. (1973) *Einführung in die Sozialpsychologie.* Weinheim.

Loudon, D. and Della Bitta, A.J. (1993) *Consumer Behavior – Concepts and Applications*, 4th Edition. New York.

Mahnkopf, D. (1969) Systematische Theorie sozialen Konsumverhaltens. Versuch einer systematischen Theorie sozialen Konsumverhaltens als allgemeine Theorie sozial-strukturell bestimmten Verhaltens ökonomischer Relevanz. Dissertation, Freiburg i. Br.

Martineau, P. (1959) *Kaufmotive*. Düsseldorf.

Maslow, A.H. (1964) A Theory of Human Motivation, in: H.J. Leavitt and L.R. Pondy (eds.), *Readings in Managerial Psychology*. Chicago/London, p. 6 ff.

Maslow, A.H. (1970) *Motivation and Personality*, 2nd Edition. New York: Harper & Row.

Mayer de Groot, R.U. (1987) *Imagetransfer*. Hamburg.

Mayer, A. and Mayer, R.U. (1987) *Imagetransfer*. Hamburg: Spiegel-Verlag.

McGuire, W.J. (1968) Nature of Attitudes and Attitude Change, in: *Handbook of Social Psychology*. New York.

McNeal, J.U. (1969) *Dimensions of Consumer Behavior*. New York.

Meffert, H. (1988) Markenstrategien als Waffe im Wettbewerb, in: H. Henzler (ed.), *Handbuch Strategische Führung*. Wiesbaden, pp. 581–610.

Meffert, H. and Heinemann, G. (1990) Operationalisierung des Imagetransfers, *Marketing ZEP*, **12** (1), 5–10.

Meffert, H. and Schürmann, U. (1991) *Werbung und Markterfolg – eine empirische Untersuchung auf der Grundlage von Experteneinschätzungen im Markenartikelbereich*. Münster: Gemeinschaftsstudie von Institut für Marketing, GWA and A.C. Nielsen GmbH.

Ogilvy, D. (1979) *Was ich von der Werbung gelernt habe; Vortrag auf dem 1. Deutschen Kommunikationstag und BDW-Kongreß*. Berlin.

Parsons, T. and Shils, E.A. (1951) *Toward a General Theory of Action*. Cambridge/MA.

Pawlik, K. (1968) *Dimensionen des Verhaltens*. Bern/Stuttgart.

Reeves, R. (1963) *Werbung ohne Mythos*. München.

Reeves, R. (1969) *Reality in Advertising*. New York, 1960. *Werbung ohne Mythos*. München.

Reiter, G. (1991) Strategien des Imagetransfers, *Jahrbuch der Absatz- und Verbrauchsforschung*, **37** (3), 210–222.

Rieke, R.D. and Sillars, M.O. (1975) *Argumentation and the Decision Making Process*. New York/London/Sydney/Toronto.

Rokeach, M. (1967) Attitude Change and Behavioral Change, *Public Opinion Quarterly*, **30**.

Roselius, T. (1977) Consumer Ranking of Risk Reduction Methods, *Journal of Marketing*, **35** (January), 56–61.

Rosenstiel, L. von (1969) *Psychologie der Werbung*. Rosenheim.

Rossiter, J.R. and Percy, L. (1987) *Advertising and Promotion Management*. New York: McGraw-Hill.

Schiffman, L.G. and Kanuk, L. (1994) *Consumer Behavior*, 5th Edition. London, u.a.

Schirner, M. (1988) *Werbung ist Kunst*. München.

Schramm, W. (1954) *The Process and Effects of Mass Communication*. Urbana, IL: University of Illinois Press.

Schulz, R. (1972) *Kaufentscheidungsprozesse des Konsumenten*. Wiesbaden.

Schulz, R. and Brandmeyer, K. (1989) *Marken-Bilanz: Das Markenbewertungssystem*. Nielsen Marketing Research.

Settle, R.B. and Alreck, P.L. (1986) *Why They Buy – American Consumers Inside and Out*. New York u.a.

Sheth, J.N. (1974) *Models of Buyer Behavior. Conceptual, Quantitative and Empirical*. New York u.a.

Six, B. (1983) Effektivität der Werbung, in: Irle (1983), 2. Halbbd., pp. 341–386.

Smith, G.H. (1954) *Motivation Research in Advertising and Marketing*. New York: McGraw-Hill.

Söllner, W.J. (ca. 1975) *Modelle zur Werbewirkungsprognose für Konsumgüter – Markenartikel; Gruner + Jahr*. Schriftenreihe Bd. 19. Hamburg o.J.

Sollwedel, I. (1978) Appelle an Träume und Triebe – Mutterliebe durch Babypuder. Konsum als weibliche Lebenserfüllung, *Publik*, No. 11, 2 July.

*Spiegel* (1997) Issue 37/97.

Steffenhagen, H. (1976) Markenbekanntheit als Werbeziel, *Zeitschrift für Betriebswirtschaft*, **46** (10), 715–734.

Steffenhagen, H. (1978) *Wirkungen absatzpolitischer Instrumente. Theorie und Messung der Marktreaktion*. Stuttgart.

Thomae, H. (ed.) (1965) *Die Motivation menschlichen Handelns*. Köln/Berlin.

Todt, E. *et al.* (eds.) (1977) *Motivation*. Heidelberg.

Todt, E. u.a. (1977) *Motivation*. Stuttgart.

Trommsdorff, V. (1993) *Konsumentenverhalten*, 2nd Edition. Stuttgart.

Walker, C. (1995) How Strong Is Your Brand, *Marketing Tools*, January/February, 46–53.

Watzlawick, P., Beavin, J.H. and Jackson, D.D. (1969) *Menschliche Kommunikation – Formen, Störungen, Paradoxien*. 7th Unchanged Edition. Bern.

Watzlawick, P., Beavin, J.H. and Jackson, D.D. (1985) *Menschliche Kommunikation*. Bern/Stuttgart/Wien.

Watzlawick, P., Weakland, J. and Fisch, R. (1974) *Lösungen – Zur Theorie und Praxis menschlichen Wandels*, 4th Edition. Bern.

Weiner, B. (1988) *Motivationspsychologie*, 2nd Edition. Munich.

Weiner, B. (1992) *Human Motivation: Metaphors, Theories and Research*. Newbury Park u.a.

Wilkie, W.L. (1990) *Consumer Behavior*, 2nd Edition. New York: John Wiley & Sons.

Wilkie, W.L. (1994) *Consumer Behavior*, 3rd Edition. New York: John Wiley & Sons.

Wiswede, G. (1990) Motivation des Kaufverhaltens, in: Hoyos, Kroeber-Riel *et al.* 2nd Edition.

Yovovich, B.G. (1988) What Is Your Brand Really Worth? *Adweek's Marketing Week*, August 8.

Yovovich, B.G. (1988) Hit and Run: Cadillac's Costly Mistake, *Adweek's Marketing Week*, August 8, p. 24.

ZAW (1997) *Werbung in Deutschland 1997*. Bonn.

# BENEFITS & PROMISES

Aronson, E., Turner, J.A. and Carlsmith, J.M. (1963) Communicator Credibility and Communication Discrepancy as Determinants of Opinion Change, *Journal of Abnormal and Social Psychology*, **67**, 31–36.

Baseheart, J. and Miller, G.R. (1969) Source Trustworthiness, Opinionated Statements, and Response to Persuasive Communication, *Speech Monographs*, **1**, 1–7.

Bochner, St. and Insko, Ch.A. (1966) Communicator Discrepancy, Source Credibility, and Opinion Change, *Journal of Personality and Social Psychology*, **4**, 614–621.

Burda GmbH (eds.) (1996) *Typologie der Wünsche – Strukturen von Zielgruppen und deren Kommunikationsverhalten*. Offenburg.

Di Vesta, F.J. and Merwin, K.W. (1953) Complex Learning and Conditioning as a Function of Anxiety, *Journal of Experimental Psychology*, **45**, 120–125.

Dieterle, G. (1992) *Die Suche nach verhaltenswirksamen Bildmotiven für eine erlebnisbetonte Werbung, Bd. 34 der Reihe Konsum und Verhalten*. Heidelberg.

Fine, B.J. (1954) Conclusion-Drawing, Communicator Credibility, and Anxiety as Factors in Opinion Change, *The Journal of Abnormal and Social Psychology*, **54**, 369–374.

Goldberg, M.E. and Hartwick, J. (1990) The Effects of Advertiser Reputation and Extremity of Advertising Claim on Advertising Effectiveness, *Journal of Consumer Research*, **17** (September), 172–179.

Greenberg, B.S. and Miller, G.R. (1966) The Effects of Low-Credible Sources on Message Acceptance, *Speech Monographs*, **33**, 127–136.

Hovland, C.I. and Weiss, W. (1951) The Influence of Source Credibility on Communication Effectiveness, *Public Opinion Quarterly*, **15**.

Janis, I.L. and Feshbach, S. (1953) Effects of Fear-Arousing Communications, *Journal of Abnormal and Social Psychology*, **48**. Auswirkungen angstregender Kommunikation, in: Irle (ed.): *Texte aus der experimentellen Sozialpsychologie, 1969*.

Konert, F.-J. (1986) *Vermittlung emotionaler Erlebniswerte. Eine Markenstrategie für gesättigte Märkte*. Heidelberg and Wien.

Kroeber-Riel, W. (1986) Innere Bilder – Signale für das Kaufverhalten, *Absatzwirtschaft*, **29** (1), 50–57.

Norris, D.G. (1992) Ingredient Branding: A Strategy Option with Multiple Beneficiaries, *Journal of Consumer Marketing*, **9** (3), 19–31.

Perelman, Ch. (1979) *Logik und Argumentation (Reihe: Philosophie/Wissenschaftstheorie)*. Königstein/Ts.

Powell, F.A. (1965) Source Credibility and Behavior Compliance as Determinants of Attitude Change, *Journal of Personality and Social Psychology*, **2**, 669–676.

Ries, A. and Trout, J. (1985) *Positioning: The Battle for Your Mind*. New York: McGraw-Hill Book Company.

Scheid, D. (1973) Die Verwendung von Angstappellen in der Werbung, Arbeitspapiere des Instituts für Konsum- und Verhaltensforschung im Institut für empirische Wirtschaftsforschung an der Universität des Saarlandes, Heft 24 (Juli).

Schulze, G. (1992) *Die Erlebnisgesellschaft*. Frankfurt am Main.

Silberer, G. (1990) *Werteforschung und Werteorientierung*. Stuttgart.

Weinberg, P. (1992) *Erlebnismarketing*. München.

Weinberg, P. and Gröppel, A. (1989) Emotional Benefits in Marketing Communication, *Irish Marketing Review*, **4**, 21–31.

# NORMS & VALUES

Abelson, R.P. *et al.* (eds.) (1968) *Theories of Cognitive Consistency. A Source Book*. Chicago.

Argyle, M. (1957) Social Pressure in Public and Private Situations, *Journal of Abnormal and Social Psychology*, **54**.

Aronson, E. (1994) *Sozialpsychologie. Menschliches Verhalten und gesellschaftlicher Einfluß*. Heidelberg.

Asch, S.E. (1951) Effects of Group Pressure Upon the Modification and Distortion of Judgement, in: H. Guetzkow (ed.), *Groups, Leadership, and Men*. Pittsburgh.

Bruhn, M. (1985) Das ökologische Bewußtsein der Konsumenten – Ergebnisse einer Befragung im Zeitvergleich, in H. Meffert and H. Wagner (eds.), *Ökologie und Unternehmensführung*, Arbeitspapier No. 26 der Wissenschaftlichen Gesellschaft für Marketing und Unternehmensführung, e.V. an der Universität Münster.

Fazio, R. and Zanna, M. (1981) Direct Experiences and Attitude Behavior Consistency, in: L. Berkowitz (ed.), *Advances in Experimental Social Psychology*, Vol. 14. New York: Academic Press, pp. 161–202.

Fazio, R.H., Sanbonmatsu, D.M., Powell, M.C. and Kardes, F.R. (1986) On the Automatic Activation of Attitudes, *Journal of Personality and Social Psychology*, **50** (February), 229–238.

Festinger, L. Schachter, S. and Back, K.W. (1950) *Social Pressure in Informal Groups*. New York.

Gergen, K.J. and Bauer, R.A. (1972) *Interactive Effects of Self-Esteem and Task Difficulty on Social Psychology*. New York.

Goldberg, S.C. (1954) Three Situational Determinants of Conformity to Social Norms, *Journal of Abnormal and Social Psychology*, **49**, 325–329.

Haley, J. (1988) Die Psychotherapie Milton H. Ericksons. Munich.

Hillmann, K.H. (1971) *Soziale Bestimmungsgründe des Konsumentenverhaltens*. Stuttgart.

Hoegl, S. (1989) Preisschwellen und Preispolitik, *Planung und Analyse*, **16**, 371–376.

Höger, A. (1992) Der Zusammenhang von Preis und Kaufverhalten, *Planung und Analyse*, **19**, 46–50.

Kiesler, Ch.A. (1963) Attraction to the Group and Conformity of Group Norms, *Journal of Psychology*, **31**.

Kiesler, Ch.A. (1971) *The Psychology of Commitment*. New York/London.

Lewin, K. (1958) Group Decisions and Social Change, in: E.E. Maccoby, T.M. Newcomb, and E.L. Hartley (eds.), *Readings in Social Psychology*, 3rd Edition. New York.

Maddocks, M. (1981) Conspicuous On-Consumption, *The Christian Science Monitor*, **19** (March), 22 (zit. Nach: American Council on Consumer Interests *Newsletter*, **29** (5), May 1981).

Mahnkopf, D. (1969) *Systematische Theorie sozialen Konsumverhaltens.* Mainz.

Martin, J., Lobb, B., Chapman, G.C. and Spillan, R. (1976) Obedience Under Conditions Demanding Self-Immolation, *Human Relations*, **29** (4), 345–356.

Milgram, S. (1963) Behavioral Study of Obedience, *Journal of Abnormal and Social Psychology*, **67**.

Milgram, S. (1974) *Obedience to Authority*, New York.

Moran, W.T. (1978) Insights from Pricing Research, in: E.B. Bailey (ed.), *Pricing Practices and Strategies*. New York: The Conference Board, pp. 7–13.

Pitts, R.E. and Woodside, A.G. (1984) *Personal Values & Consumer Psychology*. Lexington.

Rokeach, M. (1968) *Beliefs, Attitudes and Values*. San Franciso.

Rokeach, M. (1973) *The Nature of Human Values*. New York.

Rokeach, M. (1979) *Understanding Human Values*. London/New York.

Schürmann, P. (1988) *Werte und Konsumverhalten*. München.

Sherif, M. (1936) *The Psychology of Social Norms*, New York.

Spieker, H. (1990) *Gesellschaftliche Bedingungen umweltbewußten Konsums*, Arbeitspapier der Forschungsgruppe Konsum und Verhalten, Paderborn.

Steiner, I.D. (1968) Reactions to Adverse and Favorable Evaluations of One's Self, *Journal of Psychology*, **36**.

Sternthal, B., Dholakia, R. *et al.* (1978) The Persuasive Effect of Source Credibility: Tests of Cognitive Response, *Journal of Consumer Research*, **4** (4), 252–260.

# PERCEPTIONS & PROGRAMS

Brinton, C. (1936) *The Lives of Talleyrand*. New York, p. 190.

Carpenter, G.S. (1989) Perceptual Positioning and Competitive Strategy in a Two-Dimensional, Two-Brand Market, *Management Science*, **35** (9), 120–143.

Dieterich, M. (1986) *Konsument und Gewohnheit*. Heidelberg.

Eibl-Eibesfeld, I. (1985) *Der vorprogrammierte Mensch. Das Ererbte als bestimmender Faktor im menschlichen Verhalten.* München u.a.

Hoyer, W.D. and Brown, S.P. Effects of Brand Awareness on Choice for a Common, Repeat-Purchase Product, *Journal of Consumer Research*, **17** (September), 141–148.

Kaas, K.-P. and Dietrich, M. (1979) Die Entstehung von Kaufgewohnheiten bei Konsumgütern, *Marketing-ZFP*, **1** (1), 13–22.

Kahnemann, D. and Tverski, A. (1986) Rational Choice and the Framing of Decisions, *Journal of Business*, pp. 251–278.

Kannacher, V. (1982) *Habitualisiertes Kaufverhalten von Konsumenten.* München.

Kebeck, G. (1994) *Wahrnehmung: Theorien, Methoden und Forschungsergebnisse der Wahrnehmungspsychologie.* Weinheim.

Kroeber-Riel, W., Hemberle, G., Keitz, W. von and Wimmer, R.M. (1978) *Produktdifferenzierung durch emotionale Konditionierung.* Saarbrücken: Institut für Konsum- und Verhaltensforschung an der Universität des Saarlandes.

Mandl, H. and Gruber, H. (1993) Das träge Wissen, *Psychologie heute*, **20** (9), 64–69.

Mayer, R.U. (1984) *Produktpositionierung.* Köln.

Neumann, P. and von Rosenstiel, L. (1981) Die Positionierungsforschung für die Werbung, in: B. Tietz (ed.), *Handbuch der Werbung, Band 1: Rahmenbedingungen, Sachgebiete u. Methoden der Kommunikation und Werbung.* Landsberg am Lech, pp. 767–837.

Roth, G. (1994) *Das Gehirn und seine Wirklichkeit.* Frankfurt am Main.

Shimp, T.A. and Stuart, E.W. (1991) A Program of Classical Conditioning. Experiments Testing Variations in the Conditioned Stimulus and Context, *Journal of Consumer Research*, **18**, 1–12.

Stuart, E.W. and Shimp, T.A. (1987) Classical Conditioning of Consumer Attitudes: Four Experiments in an Advertising Context, *Journal of Consumer Research*, **14** (3), 334–349.

Warner, F. (1995) P&G. Breaking with Tradition Promotes Products as a Category, *Wall Street Journal*, April 25, B8.

Watzlawick, P. (1976) *Wie wirklich ist die Wirklichkeit?* München.

Weinberg, P. (1979) Habitualisierte Kaufentscheidungen von Konsumenten, *Die Betriebswirtschaft*, **39**, 563–571.

# IDENTITY & SELF-EXPRESSION

Aaker, J. (in press) Conceptualizing and Measuring Brand Personality, *Journal of Marketing Research*.

Adlwarth, W. (1983) *Formen und Bestimmungsgründe prestigegeleiteten Konsumverhaltens*. München.

Baudrillard, J. (1987) *Das andere Selbst*. Wien.

Bedford, J.H. von (1965) *Book of Snobs*. London.

Birdwell, A.E. (1968) A Study of the Influence of Image Congruence on Consumer Choice, *Journal of Business*, **41**, 76–88.

Broch, T.C. (1965) Communicator–Recipient Similarity and Decision Change, *Journal of Personality and Social Psychology*, **1**, 650–654.

Byrne, D. (1971) *The Attraction Paradigm*. New York: Academic Press.

Cooley, C.H. (1968) The Social Self. On the Meaning of "I", in: C. Gordon and K.J. Georgen (eds.), *The Self in Social Interaction*. New York.

Festinger, L. (1954) A Theory of Social Comparison Processes, *Human Relations*, **7**.

Fournier, S. (1995) *Understanding Consumer–Brand Relationship*. Working Paper 96-018, Harvard Business School, Harvard University, Cambridge, MA.

Goffmann, E. (1951) Symbols of Class Status; *British Journal of Sociology*, **2**.

Güttner, G. (1972) Identifikationsmodelle und Konsumverhalten; in: Bergler (ed.), *Marktpsychologie*.

Hermanns, A. (1992) Die Mode-Marke: Zur Anwendbarkeit des Markenartikelkonzeptes in der Bekleidungsmode, *Jahrbuch der Absatz- und Verbrauchsforschung*, **38** (4).

Hoffmann, H.-J. (1985) *Kleidersprache*. Frankfurt u.a.

James, F.E. (1985) I'll Wear the Coke Pants Tonight, They Go Well With My Harley-Davidson-Ring, *Wall Street Journal*, June 6, Sect. 2, 31.

Kagan, J. (1958) The Concept of Identification, *Psychology*, **65**.

Kreikebaum, H. and Rinsche, G. (1961) *Das Prestigemotiv in Konsum und Investition*. Berlin.

Lilli, W. (1978) Die Hypothesentheorie der sozialen Wahrnehmung; in: Frey (ed.), *Kognitive Theorien der Sozialpsychologie*.

Mayer, A. and Mayer, R.U. (1987) *Fach & Wissen: Imagetransfer*. Hamburg.

Mitscherlich, M. (1978) *Das Ende der Vorbilder. Vom Nutzen und Nachteil der Idealisierung*. Munich.

Murray, H. (1938) *Explorations in Personality*. New York: Oxford Book Company Inc.

Plummer, J.T. (1984/85) How Personality Makes a Difference, *Journal of Advertising Research*, **24** (December 1984/January 1985), 27–31.

Ross, I. (1971) Self-Concept and Brand Preference, *Journal of Business*, **44**, 38–50.

Schulz, W. (1990) Prestige und Konsum, *Werbeforschung & Praxis*, **4**, 127–136.

Séguéla, J. (1983) *Hollywood wäscht weißer – Werbung mit dem Starsystem*. Landsberg am Lech.

Sieverding, M. (1988) Attraktion und Partnerwahl – Geschlechtsrollenstereotype bei der Partnerwahl, *Report Psychologie*, **7**.

Sirgy, J.M. (1982) Self Concept in Consumer Behavior: A Critical Review, *Journal of Consumer Research*, **9** (December), 287–300.

Solomon, M.R. (1983) The Role of Products as Social Stimuli: A Symbolic Interactionism Perspective, *Journal of Consumer Research*, **10** (December), 319–329.

Specht, G. (1973) Selbst-Image des Konsumenten und Marketing-Management, in: K. Hax and I. Pentzlin (eds.), *Instrumente der Unternehmensführung*. München, pp. 110–128.

Veblen, Th. (1899) *The Theory of the Leisure Class*. New York.

Watzlawick, P. (1977) *Die Möglichkeit des Andersseins*. Stuttgart: Huber.

# EMOTIONS & LOVE

Allen, C.T. and Machleit, K.A. (1992) A Comparison of Attitudes and Emotions as Predictors of Behavior at Diverse Levels of Behavioral Experience, *Journal of Consumer Research*, **18** (4), 493–504.

Amelang, M. (ed.) (1991) *Attraktion und Liebe*. Göttingen.

Baudrillard, J. (1992) *Von der Verführung*. München.

Bottenberg, E.H. (1972) *Emotionspsychologie. Ein Beitrag zur empirischen Dimensionierung emotionaler Vorgänge*. München.

Buck, R. (1988) *Human Motivation and Emotion*, 2. Aufl. New York u.a.

Creel, R.E. (1983) Endology: The Science of Happiness, *New Ideas in Psychology*.

Dichter, E. (1961) *The Strategy of Desire*. New York.

Drieseberg, T.J. (1995) *Lebensstil-Forschung*. Heidelberg.

Edell, J.A. and Burke, M.C. (1987) The Power of Feelings, *Journal of Consumer Research*, **14**, 421–433.

Eibl-Eibesfeld, I. (1982) *Liebe und Hass – Zur Naturgeschichte elementarer Verhaltensweisen*. München: Piper.

Fellows, E.W. (1966) Happiness: A Survey of Research, *Journal of Humanistic Psychology*, **6**.

Fournier, S. (1996) *Understanding Consumer–Brand Relationships*, Working Paper 96-018, Harvard Business School, Harvard University, Cambridge, MA.

Friedrich, B. (1982) *Emotionen im Alltag. Versuch einer deskriptiven und funktionalen Analyse*. München: Minverva-Publikationen.

Gerhards, J. (1988) *Soziologie der Emotionen*. Weinheim u.a.

Heller, A. (1980) *Theorie der Gefühle*. Hamburg: VSA-Verlag.

Holbrook, M.B. and Batra, R. (1987) Assessing the Role of Emotions As Mediators of Consumer Responses to Advertising, *Journal of Consumer Research*, **14**, 404–420.

Izard, C.E. (1994) *Die Emotionen des Menschen: eine Einführung in die Grundlagen der Emotionspsycholgie*, 2nd Edition. Weinheim u.a.

Kirchler, E. and Hoelzl, E. (1995) Vom Austausch zum Altruismus, Profitorientierung versus spontane Angebote in interpersonellen Beziehungen, *Gruppendynamik*, **26** (4), 457–465.

Kroeber-Riel, W. (1974) Erotik verführt zum Konsum. Das verfehlte Leitbild der Verbraucherauf klärung, *Wirtschaftswoche*, **28**, 50–52.

Luhmann, N. (1982) *Liebe als Passion*. Frankfurt am Main.

Moser, K. (1997) *Sex-Appeal in der Werbung*. Göttingen.

Murstein, B.I. (1971) *Theories of Attraction and Love*. New York.

Plutchik, R. (1991) *The Emotions*, Revised Edition. Lanham u.a.

Plutchik, R. (1994) *The Psychology and Biology of Emotions*. New York u.a.

Plutchik, R. and Kellerman, H. (1989) *Emotion – Theory, Research and Experience*, Vol. 4: *The Measurement of Emotions*. San Diego u.a.

Plutchik, R. and Kellerman, H. (eds.) (1980) *Emotion – Theory, Research and Experience*. New York: Academic Press.

Rosenberg, M.J. (1960) An Analysis of Affective-Cognitive Consistency, in: M.J. Rosenberg *et al.*, *Attitude Organization and Change*. New Haven.

Scherer, K.R. (1986) On the Nature and Function of Emotion: A Component Process Approach, in: K.R. Scherer, *Vocal Affect Expression: A Review and a Model for Future Research. Psychological Bulletin*, **99**. In: Scherer & Schneider, *Funk-kolleg, Studienbegleitbrief*.

Schmidt-Atzert, L. (1981) *Emotionspsychologie*. Stuttgart u.a.: Neuauflage in Vorbereitung.

Stemmler, G. (1984) *Psychophysiologische Emotionsmuster*. Frankfurt am Main, Berlin, New York, Nancy: Lang.

Stendhal. (1994) *Über die Liebe*. Baden-Baden.

Ulich, D. (1989) *Das Gefühl – Eine Einführung in die Emotionspsychologie*, 2nd Edition. München u.a.

Ulich, D. and Mayring, P. (1992) *Psychologie der Emotionen*. Stuttgart.

Volpert, W. (1988) *Zauberlehrlinge. Die gefährliche Liebe zum Computer*. München: DTV.

## Wanted: Believers!

White Lion International AG is seeking:

- Creatives who challenge the conventional
- Strategic Planners who want to work with growth codes
- Entrepreneurs who want to build our international subsidiaries

Interested? Please contact Andreas Buchholz

**+49 (0) 6172-6828-0**

WHITE LION International AG
Branch Bad Homburg
Ferdinandstaße 18
D-61348 Bad Homburg v.d.h.
Tel.: (49) 6172-6828-0
Fax: (49) 6172-6828-68
e-mail: A.Buchholz@white-lion.de
Internet: www.white-lion.com

# INDEX